lonely planet
kids

ROME
City Trails

Moira Butterfield

WIN HERE!

TAKE THE STAGE

GREEN ROME

WALK, SHOP, WALK
PARTY DAYS
ROME'S GHOSTIE GUESTS

GOING GRUESOME

DELICIOUS ROME

SPOTTED OUTSIDE

WEAR ROME

MEET THE CREATURES

WHERE EMPERORS TROD

THE HOLY WAY

LOOK UP

I'M IN CHARGE

LOOK DOWN

BRILLIANT BUILDINGS
WATERY ROME

ANDIAMO!

Hi... we're Amelia and Marco and we've created 19 awesome themed trails for you to follow.

The pins on this map mark the starting points, and each trail is packed with secrets, stories and lots of other cool stuff. So whether you are a foodie, a sports fanatic or a history buff, this book has got something for you!

CONTENTS

WHERE EMPERORS TROD

There's so much history in Rome that walking round it can feel like time travelling. Start your Roman adventure by taking a trail back over 2,000 years to the Forum at the heart of Ancient Rome. The Roman Empire ruled most of Europe, the Middle East and northern Africa for hundreds of years until the city finally fell to its enemies in the fifth century AD.

TOP ROMAN ROAD

VIA SACRA

This road runs through the Forum, surrounded by the remains of temples and other important ancient buildings. The paving slabs on the road have survived for 2,000 years, so today's visitors walk along in the footsteps of the Ancient Romans. When Roman generals won great battles they were sometimes allowed to lead a huge parade called a triumph along the Via Sacra. Treasures brought back from conquered lands would be paraded before the crowds in the victory march, along with chained-up prisoners.

VIA SACRA

SHOW-OFF STONE

ARCH OF TITUS

The Arch of Titus is a triumphal arch, built to celebrate military victories. It shows Roman soldiers parading valuables captured from the Jewish kingdom of Judea in the Middle East in the first century AD. Rome was ruled at that time by the emperor Titus, and the arch is a kind of giant stone advert for his greatness.

ARCH OF TITUS

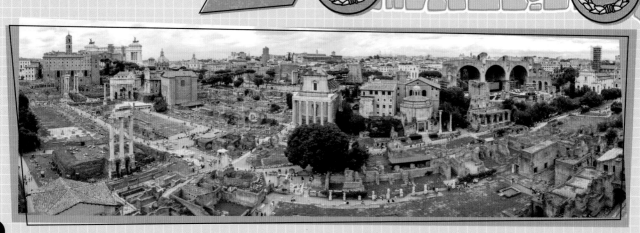

CROWDS RAN FROM CAESAR'S FUNERAL LOOKING FOR HIS MURDERERS. THEY KILLED A MAN THEY THOUGHT WAS ONE OF CAESAR'S ENEMIES, AND PARADED HIS HEAD ON A SPEAR, BUT THEY KILLED THE WRONG PERSON.

THE CURIA

ROME'S RULING HOUSE

THE CURIA

Government VIPs called senators sat in the Senate at the Curia to debate Roman laws. It would have been easy to spot them because they dressed in togas decorated with a broad purple stripe, and wore natty red ankle boots. Being a senator brought power but also danger – from time to time senators were murdered for disagreeing with Rome's emperors! Modern US senators are named after these Ancient Roman governors.

HAIL CAESAR

TEMPLE OF JULIUS CAESAR

When Ancient Roman ruler Julius Caesar was stabbed to death by his enemies in 44 BC, his remains were brought to this spot and burnt on a pyre, while his blood-stained tunic was displayed nearby. Soldiers threw weapons onto the flames to honour their dead leader, women threw jewellery and some people even ripped up their robes and threw the pieces on the fire. After his death, Caesar was declared a god and a temple was built in his honour on the spot where he was cremated.

TEMPLE OF JULIUS CAESAR

SATURN'S SPOT
TEMPLE OF SATURN

The Ancient Romans worshipped lots of gods and goddesses. Each one had their own temple. This one was dedicated to the god Saturn, who has given his name to the English word 'Saturday'. *Saturnalia* was a popular midwinter festival celebrated by the whole of Rome, when everyone partied and gave gifts in honour of Saturn. Later, the Saturnalia festivities were ended by the Christian church, whose followers began celebrating Christmas instead. The Temple of Saturn was also the State Treasury, where piles of gold and silver were stored.

"Friends, Romans, countrymen, lend me your ears."

HAPPY SATURDAY

SPEAK UP, SENATOR!
THE ROSTRA

This was the stage where Rome's politicians made speeches to the crowds. In the Shakespeare play *Julius Caesar*, Marc Antony stands up here to make the famous speech that begins: 'Friends, Romans, countrymen, lend me your ears.' For Roman senator Cicero the part about the ears came all too true. When he was executed for quarrelling with his superiors, his right hand and his head (including ears) were displayed here. Gruesome!

THE SPEECH PLATFORM GOT ITS NAME FROM THE SHIP PROWS (FRONT ENDS) CAPTURED FROM DEFEATED ENEMIES AND PUT ON DISPLAY HERE. THEY WERE CALLED *ROSTRA*.

GIRLS ONLY

HOUSE OF THE VESTALS

The Vestal Virgins lived here in Ancient Roman times. They were priestesses in white robes, whose job it was to keep a flame continually burning in the nearby Temple of Vesta, goddess of the home. They made cakes to offer to the goddess, too. Girls aged six to ten were selected to live in the house and become priestesses for the next 30 years. When they entered for the first time they had all their hair cut off and hung on a tree outside the house as an offering to the gods.

TEMPLE OF CASTOR AND POLLUX

TOP TWINS

TEMPLE OF CASTOR AND POLLUX

Twins will be pleased to know that among the Roman gods and goddesses there were two handsome twin brothers called Castor and Pollux. These two brilliant boys got their own temple in the Forum because they apparently appeared on magical white horses during an important battle, leading the Romans to victory. They appeared again with their horses in the Forum and their temple was later built on that spot.

search: CASTOR AND POLLUX

⦿ STARRING ROLE

You can still see these Roman twins if you look up at the night sky. Legend has it that they never wanted to be separated, so their father – Jupiter, king of the gods – turned them into the brightest two stars in the constellation of Gemini.

VESTAL VIRGINS WERE IMPORTANT AND POWERFUL WOMEN IN ROME. BUT ANY VESTAL VIRGIN WHO LET THE SACRED FIRE GO OUT WAS IN FOR A HARSH PUNISHMENT, AND ANY VESTAL VIRGIN WHO SECRETLY GOT A BOYFRIEND COULD BE BURIED ALIVE!

HOUSE OF THE VESTALS

UPTOWN TOP-RANKING

THE PALATINE HILL

The Palatine Hill above the Forum is the place where Rome was said to have been founded. Later it was where the Roman emperors lived in grand palace luxury. It may have been the top spot in town in toga-wearing times, but nowadays it's a great place for picnicking in the shade while gazing at the ruins.

753 BC

THE YEAR ROME IS SAID TO HAVE BEEN FOUNDED.

The length of time Emperor Domitian's home served as the main imperial palace.

300 YEARS

THE BEST DECORATORS

It was Emperor Augustus who first set up home here. Some of the wall paintings in his house can still be seen today, including garden plants and animals on the walls of a dining room. Augustus's wife, Livia, was accused by some of being a plant expert, but not in a good way. They said she was a murderess who used poison from plants to kill anyone she didn't like, including Augustus!

DOMITIAN'S MYSTERY

Next to his palace (the Domus Flavia) Emperor Domitian built a walled area called the Stadium. It looks like a big running track but nobody knows what it was really for. It could have been for exercising the emperor's horses or perhaps just for taking a stroll. We'll never know, so take a guess. Like both Caesar and Caligula, Domitian was killed by his enemies. In Roman times there was a high body count on the Palatine Hill!

ROME STARTS WITH A FIGHT!

ACCORDING TO ROMAN MYTHOLOGY, TWIN BABY BROTHERS ROMULUS AND REMUS WERE FOUND FLOATING IN A BASKET ON THE RIVER TIBER BY A SHE-WOLF. SHE TOOK THEM TO A CAVE ON THE PALATINE NOW KNOWN AS THE *LUPERCAL* (WOLF CAVE). WHEN THEY WERE OLDER, ROMULUS DECIDED TO BUILD A CITY CALLED ROME ON THE HILL, BUT HIS BROTHER DISAGREED AND THERE WAS A TERRIBLE QUARREL. ROMULUS KILLED REMUS AND WENT ON TO BUILD THE CITY JUST WHERE HE WANTED IT.

DOMUS FLAVIA

STADIUM

SAINT IN THE STADIUM

Many churches in Rome contain paintings of St. Sebastian, a Christian Roman soldier who was killed on the orders of Emperor Diocletian. According to legend he was tied to a tree in the Stadium and shot full of arrows. Somehow he survived and appeared later in front of the astonished emperor to tell him what an awful man he was. Then Sebastian really was killed, this time he was hit with clubs, but paintings usually show him tied to the tree and pierced with arrows.

DELICIOUS ROME

Warning! This tasty trail will make you feel hungry because Rome is a city full of yummy food. There's sweet cool gelato and crunchy pizza, golden pasta and chocolate so wonderful that it has had poems written about it. *'Mangia!'* as they say in Italy, 'Eat!'

START

PIAZZA NAVONA

ROMA vs NAPOLI
~*~*~*~

PIZZA IS SAID TO HAVE BEEN INVENTED IN NAPLES AS FOOD FOR THE POOR, BUT ROME HAS ITS OWN VERSION. THE NAPLES PIZZA IS PUFFIER AND SOFTER THAN THE THINNER AND CRISPIER ROMAN PIZZA. NEVER GET INTO A DISCUSSION WITH LOCAL PEOPLE ABOUT WHICH TYPE IS BEST. PIZZA PASSIONS RUN HIGH HERE!

WITCHY SWEETS

PIAZZA NAVONA CHRISTMAS MARKET

On the Christian *Eve of the Epiphany* (6 January), the good witch Befana is said to travel around Italy delivering sweets to children who have been good. Naughty children get a lump of coal instead. In Rome, Befana would be most likely to get her stock of sugary treats from the sweet stalls at the Piazza Navona Christmas Market.

PERFECT PIZZA

ALL OVER ROME

Here's a brief guide to the Roman pizza snacks sold everywhere around town. First up, there's *pizza al taglio* – rectangular slices of pizza cooked in a big tray. Then there's *pizza bianca*, which means 'white pizza'. These slices don't have any tomato sauce on them, just olive oil. *Pizza bianca* is also sold as *pizza farcita*, with delicious fillings inside. Got that? Now go munch some!

ALL OVER ROME

POETRY IN CHOCOLATE

MORIONDO & GARIGLIO

Romans having been tucking into gorgeous Moriondo & Gariglio goodies for around 150 years. It's the city's oldest chocolatier, with over 100 varieties of melt-in-the-mouth chocolates and bonbons. At Easter there are big queues for its beautiful Easter eggs, especially the ones filled with velvety *gianduia* – a chocolate hazelnut spread similar to Nutella® but even better.

"Hello?"

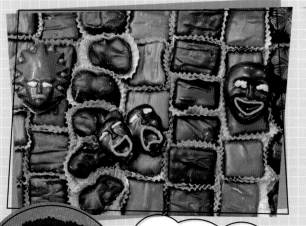

"It's a welcome gift that makes a child happy, and should you travel the whole world you'll only find it at Moriondo's."

TRILUSSA, A FAMOUS ROMAN POET, WAS SO IMPRESSED BY THIS SHOP THAT HE DEDICATED SEVERAL POEMS TO IT. THESE ARE SOME LINES FROM A POEM CELEBRATING ONE OF ITS CHOCOLATES.

FRIED TELEPHONES

RIONE DI SANT'ANGELO

Jewish people were once confined to this area of Rome, so it became known as the Jewish Ghetto. Here they developed a style of cooking that made the best of the inexpensive ingredients they could afford. Deep-fried rice, tomato and mozzarella balls called *supplì al telefono* (telephone surprises) originated here. Pull a *supplì* apart and you'll see a 'telephone wire' – a delicious string of melted mozzarella stretching between the two halves.

Some more Roman Jewish Ghetto specialities

PIZZA EBRAICA – a cookie-like bar full of nuts, raisins and candied fruit.

CARCIOFI ALLA GIUDIA – deep-fried artichokes.

BACCALÀ – deep-fried codfish.

CONCIA – deep-fried and pickled courgettes.

GELATO PLEASE!

IL GELATO DI CLAUDIO TORCÈ

Gelato isn't just any old ice cream. It's tastier and thicker. It's sold all over Rome – just make sure you seek out an authentic handmade *gelato* using fresh ingredients. Claudio Torcè has become famous for creating unusual flavours such as celery and cheese, as well as delicious sweet treats.

2,500
APPROX. NUMBER OF GELATERIE (ICE CREAM SHOPS) IN ROME

Stracciatella
(vanilla with chocolate flakes) and ***gianduia*** (chocolate and hazelnut) are traditional flavours.

GRATTACHECCA
= SHAVINGS OF ICE
FLAVOURED WITH SYRUP

NO LEFTOVERS HERE

TESTACCIO

This area of Rome once had lots of abattoirs, where animals were killed for meat. The parts that nobody wanted went to the workers, which is how *cucina romana* (Roman cooking) came about. It uses things you wouldn't normally find on your plate, such as animal heads, hearts, lungs, feet and stomach parts. A rich oxtail stew, *coda alla vaccinara*, is a typical example of Roman cooking. It's made from the tail of a cow.

TESTACCIO

14

1,262M² (13,580FT²)

The total surface area of the world's largest pizza, made in Rome in 2012.

AL DENTE

This is the traditional way to cook pasta in Italy. *Dente* means tooth (think dentist) and *al dente* describes they way pasta should feel when you bite into it. Nobody likes soggy pasta!

ALL OVER ROME

WINTERTIME IN ROME

CALDARROSTAI

The *caldarrostai* sell delicious roasted chestnuts, freshly cooked on portable street roasters around town. Chestnuts come into season in October and November in the countryside around Rome, which is when you'll see the *caldarrostai*. A paper cone of hot chestnuts is a great way to warm up your hands and your tummy when it's cold in the capital.

NEVER CREAM!

SPAGHETTI CARBONARA

Spaghetti carbonara is probably Rome's favourite pasta dish. It's made of spaghetti with egg sauce, grated cheese and pieces of cured pork. Everyone argues over how it was invented. Some think it was first made by local miners as a campfire food. Others say it was invented by people using Second World War rations. They all agree on one thing though. Nobody in Rome would EVER add cream to the recipe. That would be *scioccante* – shocking!

ALL OVER ROME

WATERY ROME

Rome has water at its heart. It was built on the River Tiber and is full of beautiful fountains, which are especially welcome spots in the heat of an Italian summer. Come for a refreshing water ride through the city and beyond to find out how water has been making a splash here throughout history.

87KM (54 MILES)
DISTANCE WATER TRAVELLED FROM APENNINE MOUNTAINS

1,682 LITRES (370 GALLONS) A SECOND
RATE OF WATER FLOW
= 7x

TOILET TALK

OSTIA ANTICA

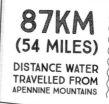

Ostia Antica used to be an important port for nearby Rome. Its archaeological remains include a great set of Ancient Roman public loos. The Ancient Romans thought nothing of pooing alongside each other, sharing one long stone bench over a channel of running water beneath. Slaves would hand them a sponge-stick or some rags for wiping as they sat chatting, perhaps even talking business as they did their business!

OSTIA ANTICA

WALK BY THE WATER

PARCO DEGLI ACQUEDOTTI

When the River Tiber became too polluted to drink in Ancient Roman times, clever engineers built aqueducts to bring fresh, clean water to the city from miles away. In this park it's possible to walk alongside stretches of an original aqueduct. Imagine the water flowing along the top towards the city, where Ancient Roman slaves might be busy washing togas, senators might be enjoying their baths and the emperor himself might be sitting giving orders by a palace fountain!

PARCO DEGLI ACQUEDOTTI

MEGA-BATHS
TERME DI CARACALLA

These ruins were once huge public baths where Ancient Romans could relax. Not only could they take cold baths, lukewarm baths, hot baths and saunas here, they could swim in an Olympic-sized pool, play ball games and work out with weights. They could buy snacks, go shopping, have a drink, play board games, visit the library and even take a look in a museum. It was rather like a big city shopping centre based on bathing.

ANCIENT ROMANS PREFERRED TO GET RID OF THEIR BODY HAIR. THEY PAID PLUCKERS TO PULL IT OUT AT THE BATHS. OUCH!

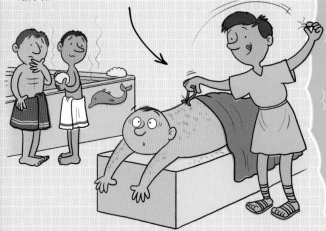

BEHIND THE SCENES, THE BATHS WERE RUN BY SLAVES. HUNDREDS OF THE UNLUCKIEST ONES SWEATED IN CELLARS BELOW THE BUILDING, FEEDING FURNACES WITH WOOD TO KEEP THE BATHWATER ABOVE NICE AND WARM.

TERME DI CARACALLA

TIBER ISLAND

MINI MEDICINE MOUND
TIBER ISLAND

One of the world's smallest inhabited islands, the *Isola Tiberina* (Tiber Island), sits in the middle of the River Tiber in Rome. For thousands of years it's been associated with healing, and there's still a hospital there. The whole island is about the size of three football pitches laid end to end.

search: ROMAN MEDICINE

📍 DOCTOR HISS

The story goes that there was once a plague in Ancient Rome, so the Romans sent a ship to Greece, to the temple of the god of medicine. They brought back one of the temple's lucky sacred snakes and it slithered onto Tiber Island from the ship, bringing with it healing powers.

OVERNIGHT TURTLES

TURTLE FOUNTAIN

Legend has it that a local duke had this Turtle Fountain built overnight to impress his future father-in-law. It's over 400 years old and is much loved because it shows four young men gently pushing turtles up into the water above. The fountain isn't all it seems, though. The turtles are copies. Three of the originals are in a museum, and a fourth was stolen by a spoilsport turtle-snatcher.

FREE DRINKS FOR EVERYONE

NASONI

There are around 2,500 cast iron drinking fountains around Rome, providing free, clean drinking water for everyone. They're nicknamed *nasoni*, meaning big noses, because of their spouts. It's completely safe to drink their fresh, cool water, and if you put your thumb over the spout, the water will shoot out of the top as a handy drinking fountain.

ALL OVER CENTRE OF ROME

BERNINI'S BIG RIVERS

FONTANA DEI QUATTRO FIUMI

This grand fountain, built in 1651 by Gian Lorenzo Bernini, celebrates what were thought of as the four greatest rivers in the world. The gods of the Ganges, the Rio de la Plata, the Danube and the Nile all sit on the fountain along with animals and plants from their homelands. The mysterious god of the Nile has his head covered by a cloth because the source of his river was still unknown.

"I can't look at it, it's so horrible!"

LEGEND HOLDS THAT ONE OF THE FIGURES ON THE FOUNTAIN IS SHIELDING HIS EYES TO AVOID LOOKING AT A NEARBY CHURCH DESIGNED BY BERNINI'S HATED RIVAL, BORROMINI. WE DO KNOW THAT THE TWO COULDN'T STAND EACH OTHER, BUT THE LEGEND IS PROBABLY JUST A JOKE.

PIAZZA NAVONA

WALL OF WATER

FLOOD MARKERS

Plaques on the wall of the Basilica di Santa Maria Sopra Minerva mark the height of the River Tiber when it has flooded over the years. The oldest plaque marks a flood that happened nearly 600 years ago. Nowadays, hydroelectric dams and protective walls along the river reduce the risk of disastrous floods.

THE HIGHEST FLOOD ON THE PLAQUES TOOK PLACE IN 1598. THE WATER ROSE 19.56M (64FT) ABOVE SEA LEVEL, WHICH WOULD BE OVER 4M (12FT) ABOVE TODAY'S STREETS.

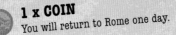

TREVI FOUNTAIN

FOUNTAIN OF FORTUNE

TREVI FOUNTAIN

Rome's most famous fountain is huge and takes up one whole side of a small square. According to legend if you throw a coin into the water you will return to Rome one day.

COIN COLLECTION

Roughly €3,000 (£2,500) is thrown into the fountain each day. It's illegal to steal a coin from the waters. The money is collected every night and used by a Roman charity to help buy food for those in need. The tradition is to throw a coin over your shoulder into the water, and the number you throw in will affect your luck in the future...

1 x COIN
You will return to Rome one day.

2 x COINS
You will find love.

3 x COINS
You will get married.

BLOOD BATH?

In 2007, onlookers got a big surprise when the fountain began to run red. Someone had secretly tipped a bucket of red dye into the water. He claimed he was an artist seeking to add colour to people's lives. Some locals were angry while others admired the artwork.

BAROQUE ROCKS

The style of the fountain is Baroque (pronounced ba-rock). It is a type of art that is full of drama and complicated details, and it was a very popular style in the 1700s when the fountain was designed.

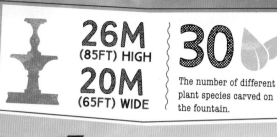

26M (85FT) HIGH
20M (65FT) WIDE

30
The number of different plant species carved on the fountain.

BLACK DAY

THE FOUNTAIN WAS AN IMPORTANT LOCATION IN A FAMOUS ITALIAN FILM CALLED *LA DOLCE VITA*. WHEN ITS STAR, MARCELLO MASTROIANNI, DIED IN 1996 THE FOUNTAIN WAS TURNED OFF AND DRAPED IN BLACK AS A TRIBUTE TO HIM. IN THE MOVIE THERE IS A FAMOUS SCENE WHEN HE WALKS INTO THE WATERS OF THE FOUNTAIN TO KISS THE ACTRESS ANITA EKBERG. NOWADAYS NOBODY PADDLES, THOUGH. SECURITY GUARDS ARE ON HAND 24 HOURS A DAY TO STOP ANYONE TRYING TO DIP THEIR TOOTSIES IN THE TREVI.

"Look again, that's not me!"

WRONG GOD?

Spectators often mistake the main fountain statue, Oceanus, for the sea god Neptune. Oceanus was a Greek god whereas Neptune was Roman. You can tell them apart because Neptune always carries a three-pronged trident.

SPOTTED OUTSIDE

"Pssst... Have you heard...?"

You're never alone in Rome! Just around the corner there's likely to be a statue or a wall carving of someone, and although the city's street statues aren't exactly chatty, they are full of surprising stories. Step this way to discover some of their stony secrets.

START

CAMPO DE' FIORI

DON'T MENTION THE ALIENS

GIORDANO BRUNO

This sinister-looking hooded monk represents Giordano Bruno, who met a grisly end on this spot in 1600. He was burnt at the stake by the Catholic Church for his beliefs, which included the idea that there might be other planets in the universe with life on them. His statue was put up in 1889 as a protest against the censorship of ideas. Perhaps it should be looking up instead of down, to spot UFOs.

WHAT DID THAT STONE SAY?

PASQUINO

Some of Rome's statues talk, and they're especially good at gossip and scandal. Actually they're statues where locals have occasionally taken to leaving anonymous notes for everyone to read, especially useful as a way to criticize Rome's rulers or gossip about neighbours without risking revenge. Pasquino is the most famous 'talking statue' but there are others, and they've even been known to 'talk' to each other across town via notes left stuck on the stones!

PIAZZA PASQUINO

CARTOON COLUMN

TRAJAN'S COLUMN

This column is covered with a 2,000-year-old cartoon. It was carved to celebrate Emperor Trajan's victories, and pictures telling the story of his war in Dacia (the name for modern day Romania and Moldova) spiral up the column. Nothing gets left out – among the scenes there are Roman soldiers building forts and crossing rivers, killing their enemies, being killed themselves and even sitting around having dull-looking meetings to discuss their next moves.

VIA DEL PIÈ DI MARMO

TOP TOES

PIÈ DI MARMO

Locals love this random-looking giant left foot, which lives in 'Marble Foot Street' and is about the size of a Fiat 500 car. It was once part of a statue of an Ancient Egyptian goddess called Isis, goddess of nature and magic. Her Ancient Roman temple was nearby but these days only her much-worn marble tootsie remains.

search: ROMAN STATUES

IT'S ALL GREEK TO ME

Lots of Roman statues are copies of Greek ones because Roman warriors brought home gorgeous Greek art. This became very popular with the Ancient Romans who asked for replicas to be made. Some statues are exact copies but others combine Greek bodies with Roman heads!

2,662 FIGURES ON THE COLUMN

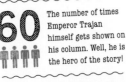

60

The number of times Emperor Trajan himself gets shown on his column. Well, he is the hero of the story!

185 STEPS INSIDE THE COLUMN

PIAZZA VENEZIA

HAIRY HORSEMAN

KING VITTORIO EMANUELE II AND IL VITTORIANO

You can't miss the giant statue of Vittorio Emanuele II. He's standing near one of Rome's busiest roundabouts in front of a huge white building called Il Vittoriano.

THE BUILDING BEHIND

THE STATUE'S BACKDROP IS A BUILDING CALLED IL VITTORIANO. LOCALS SOMETIMES CALL IT 'THE TYPEWRITER' OR 'THE WEDDING CAKE'. IT REPRESENTS THE GLORY OF ITALY AND IS PACKED FULL OF MESSAGES. THE STATUES AND CARVINGS ALL REPRESENT DIFFERENT THINGS, FROM UNITY AND LIBERTY (THE TWO SCULPTURES ON THE TOP) TO 16 ITALIAN CITIES (THE COLUMNS).

A FIRST FATHER

The king's statue and the huge white marble building behind it were built to celebrate Italy becoming a unified country in 1861, with Rome as its capital. Before that time it was a group of separate states. Vittorio Emanuele was the new nation's first king and considered its 'father' by some.

0.5M (19.5IN)
WIDTH OF THE HORSE'S HOOF.

12M (40FT)
HEIGHT OF THE STATUE

HEAD AND HELMET = SAME WEIGHT AS A YOUNG ELEPHANT!

MOUSTACHE MAN

Vittorio Emanuele was called the 'Gentleman King' or the 'Robber King', depending on whether people liked him or not. We are going to call him the best 'Moustache King' ever! His moustache was far wider than his face and he sometimes waxed the tips like an impressively hairy hipster.

MEAL FIT FOR A KING!

When the statue was first erected in 1911, it's said that 21 workmen put a table inside it and ate their lunch there.

MY TALL TREE
(BUT NOT AS TALL AS ME)

Every Christmas, Vittorio Emanuele gets to look down on one of the tallest Christmas trees in Rome, placed in the piazza in front of him.

COOL, CURLY AND ON COINS

MARCUS AURELIUS

PIAZZA DEL CAMPIDOGLIO

This horseman is Marcus Aurelius, said to be one of Ancient Rome's best emperors. Apparently he wasn't mad or bad (like most of Rome's emperors) and it's obvious that he had a great curly hairdo. Look on Italy's €0.50 coin to see a picture of the famous statue of him on his horse. What do you think the emperor is pointing at with his hand? Could he be saying, 'Move! Horse coming through!' or, 'Give me a lick of your ice cream!' perhaps?

SANTA MARIA IN ARACOELI

SANTA BAMBINO

SANTA MARIA IN ARACOELI

This wooden statue of the baby Jesus is said to have healing powers and to answer the prayers of children. Children sometimes write to the statue. Their letters are kept in the statue's chapel and then burnt to waft their prayers to heaven. At Christmas, children visit the baby.

"Waaah!"

IN 1994, THE SANTA BAMBINO STATUE WAS STOLEN, PROBABLY FOR ITS VALUABLE JEWELS. IT'S BEEN REPLACED, BUT THE NEW ONE IS STILL CONSIDERED HOLY.

2.6M HIGH (8.5FT)
HEAD OF COLOSSUS **STATUE**

10.7M (35FT) HIGH
ESTIMATED HEIGHT OF COMPLETE **STATUE**

BIG BITS

COLOSSUS OF CONSTANTINE

Emperor Constantine once had his own giant 'colossus' statue. Now all he has are a head, arm, hand, knee, two feet and a piece of thigh. His remaining statue fragments still look impressive though, with the biggest toenails and chin dimple you'll ever see. Tourists love to be photographed pointing alongside his massive finger. It's thought possible that he may have recycled somebody else's statue and had the head remodelled. It might even have started off as the statue of his enemy Maxentius, who he overthrew as emperor.

WORLD'S OLDEST LIE DETECTOR

BOCCA DELLA VERITÀ

This weird-looking wall-mounted face, with its hollow eyes and gaping mouth, is a movie star. It's appeared in several famous Rome-based films and in the *Tomb Raider Chronicles* video game, too. Its fame is down to the legend that if you put your hand in its mouth and tell a lie, it will bite your hand off. It's around 2,000 years old and is thought to represent a mysterious river, sea or forest god.

LOOK UP

It's time to explore Rome's rooftops. Look up in this city and you'll see some of the world's most famous views along with some high-up surprises.

START

VILLA DEL PRIORATO DI MALTA

PIAZZA VENEZIA

THROUGH THE KEYHOLE

VILLA DEL PRIORATO DI MALTA

People can be seen peering through the keyhole of this green villa door every day. They're not trying to spy on the Knights of Malta, the religious group who own the villa and garden. They're looking at what is said to be Rome's best view – the Dome of St. Peter's perfectly framed by the keyhole.

THIS IS WHAT
SHE IS LOOKING AT!

ROME DOMES ALL AROUND

IL VITTORIANO LIFT

Remember the Il Vittoriano building on page 24, home of the hairy horseman? At the side of the building you can take a glass lift up to a terrace where you can see a unique 360° view of the whole of Rome through the powerful telescopes provided. From there you'll soon see that Rome is a city of domes – there are lots of churches around town.

ROSE RAIN

PANTHEON

One of Rome's oldest buildings, the Pantheon, has a hole in the top. It is called an oculus, and at noon on Pentecost Sunday (a Christian festival day), Rome's firemen climb up the outside of the roof and pour red rose petals down through the hole on the people below. Originally an Ancient Roman temple, the Pantheon is now a church and the petals symbolise the Holy Spirit coming down. You can find out more about the Pantheon itself on page 92.

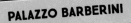

PALAZZO BARBERINI

BARBERINI BEES

PALAZZO BARBERINI

Rome has loads of amazing ceiling paintings, including a huge fresco by the artist Pietro da Cortona. It's cleverly painted to fool viewers into thinking the ceiling is much higher than it is, with fake walls and columns. Visitors are given reclining chairs to lie down on as they look at the picture and try to spot the swarm of golden bees added by the artist. The work was commissioned by the Barberini family, who had bees as their symbol.

PANTHEON

MONKEY BUSINESS
TOWER OF THE MONKEY

ANYONE WHO OWNS THE TOWER OF THE MONKEY MUST KEEP THE LAMP BURNING, OR LOSE OWNERSHIP. ITS REAL NAME IS THE TORRE DEI FRANGIPANE.

Legend has it that a medieval nobleman who lived here had a large pet monkey. One day, the monkey snatched his baby son and took it to the top of the tower. The desperate nobleman prayed to the Virgin Mary and promised to build a roof shrine with a light that burnt forever if the child was saved. The monkey came down with the baby, and the nobleman kept his promise. There is still a shrine at the top with a lamp that is turned on every night.

TOWER OF THE MONKEY

PINCIO HILL

STARS IN THEIR EYES
PINCIO VIEWING TERRACE

Every year on 10 August it's *Notte dei Desideri*, the 'Night of Wishes', and people all over Italy gather to look for shooting stars. If they see one they secretly make a wish. The shooting stars are the annual Perseid meteor shower, caused by the Swift-Tuttle comet entering Earth's atmosphere. But before people knew the science, the legend was that the stars were the tears of St. Lawrence, supposedly killed on this day. The Pincio Hill is the most popular place for the people of Rome to do their lucky star-spotting.

search: WHAT CAN YOU SEE FROM PINCIO HILL?

📍 ROMAN RACETRACK

There's a great view of Via del Corso from Pincio Terrace. This very straight street in the centre of Rome gets its name from being used as racetrack in an annual race between riderless horses called 'corsa dei barberi' during the Roman Carnival.

LIT UP WITH LENTILS

NEW YEAR'S EVE

At midnight on New Year's Eve, fireworks light up the skies of Rome for around 15 minutes. Everyone comes out to see them, having eaten their *cenone*, a big New Year's Eve dinner. But even if they're full, everyone must make sure they eat some lentils after midnight to bring fortune in the coming year. The lentils are said to look like coins.

ON NEW YEAR'S EVE YOU'LL SEE STREET STALLS AROUND TOWN SELLING RED UNDERWEAR, BECAUSE ITALIANS WEAR IT ON NEW YEAR'S EVE! THE TRADITION PROBABLY COMES FROM HUNDREDS OF YEARS AGO, WHEN RED WAS THOUGHT TO WARD OFF SICKNESS AND BAD LUCK.

24M (78FT) HIGH

CHARIOT

FLAMINIO OBELISK

The Flaminio Obelisk was brought back from Ancient Egypt over 2,000 years ago by the Roman emperor Augustus, when he defeated Cleopatra. It once stood in the Circus Maximus, Ancient Rome's chariot-racing track, where teams of charioteers thundered round it in front of cheering crowds. It came from an Egyptian temple dedicated to the sun but now it has a Christian cross on the top.

ANCIENT ROME AND EGYPT HAD A COMPLICATED RELATIONSHIP! JULIUS CAESAR HELPED CLEOPATRA TAKE CONTROL OF EGYPT. AFTER HE WAS KILLED, SHE MARRIED MARK ANTONY AND TOGETHER THEY FOUGHT OCTAVIAN. BUT OCTAVIAN (LATER CALLED AUGUSTUS) WON AND MADE EGYPT PART OF THE ROMAN EMPIRE.

UPSIDE-DOWN ART

SISTINE CHAPEL

The Sistine Chapel is in the Vatican Museums, part of the headquarters of the Catholic Church. It's where you'll find the most famous ceiling in the world, a fresco (painting on plaster) by Michelangelo. It took him four years of hard work to paint it for Pope Julius II between 1508 and 1512.

THE VATICAN

TOUGH TIME

Michelangelo painted the ceiling standing on a scaffold, craning his neck. He didn't want the job in the first place and he complained that it ruined his health. His payments were often delayed and cold damp weather stopped the plaster drying, but by the end he had made a masterpiece.

COVER—UP

In 1564, another artist was ordered to cover up some of the nude figures with fig leaves and drapery. He was given the nickname *Il Braghettone* – 'Big Pants' – by locals!

THE FRESCO STORY

MICHELANGELO'S FRESCO REPRESENTS THE BOOK OF GENESIS IN THE BIBLE, FROM THE CREATION OF THE WORLD TO THE STORY OF NOAH. THE MOST FAMOUS SECTION SHOWS GOD TOUCHING THE HAND OF ADAM, THE FIRST MAN. MICHELANGELO PAINTED GOD LAST OF ALL, BECAUSE HE THOUGHT HE WOULD BE AT HIS VERY BEST BY THEN. THE POPE WHO COMMISSIONED THE PICTURE WANTED TO SHOW THE 12 APOSTLES, BUT MICHELANGELO IGNORED HIM.

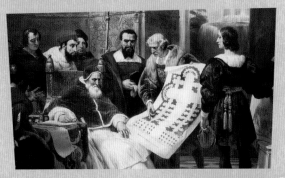

25,000

THE NUMBER OF PEOPLE WHO VISIT EVERY DAY. THAT'S 5 MILLION A YEAR.

1,110 SQ.M
(12,000SQ.FT)

THE SIZE OF THE WORK. IT'S SLIGHTLY BIGGER THAN THE SIZE OF A BASKETBALL COURT.

STAYING SAFE

The sweat, breath and even skin flakes of millions of visitors all pose a threat to the fresco, so hi-tech air conditioning has been installed to help control the room and keep damage down. Photos are banned in case the light from camera flashes fades the work.

There are plenty of secrets to be found beneath your feet in Rome, including lost homes, deadly dungeons, a mythical bull, some hidden symbols... Oh, and some slimy bird poo, too. Watch where you step!

CHRISTIAN CODE

CATACOMBS OF SAN CALLISTO

Catacombs are underground cemeteries with corridors cut through the rock and recesses for bodies. The catacombs of San Callisto were begun in Ancient Roman times when it was against the law to follow the Christian religion. Christians developed secret symbols to show their faith, and some can be seen carved on the rocks in the catacombs. The symbols include doves, fish, phoenix birds and Ancient Greek letters.

THE 'MONOGRAM OF CHRIST' APPEARS ON THE ROCKS IN THE CATACOMBS. IT IS MADE UP OF TWO LETTERS OF THE GREEK ALPHABET — CHI AND RO. THEY LOOK LIKE X AND P AND THEY ARE THE FIRST TWO LETTERS OF THE ANCIENT GREEK WORD FOR CHRIST.

SECRET SPACE

BASILICA DI SAN CLEMENTE

Excavations under this church have revealed a dark and shadowy pagan temple space from Ancient Roman times, with an altar showing the mythical god Mithras killing a bull. Those people who followed Mithras met in underground torchlit caverns and held secret ceremonies. We don't know much about them but we do know they ate ceremonial meals because they threw their food remains into a pit in their temple.

START

CATACOMBS OF SAN CALLISTO

BASILICA DI SAN CLEMENTE

GLADIATOR SCHOOL
LUDUS MAGNUS

Gladiators once trained here, then made their way by underground tunnel to the Colosseum to fight (see page 42). You can still see the small cells where around 130 rookie fighters lived while they were trained by retired gladiators. Spectators could watch them exercising or having mock fights with wooden training swords.

FEW GLADIATORS LIVED PAST THE AGE OF 30. THOSE WHO DID COULD RETIRE AS RICH AND FAMOUS CELEBRITIES. NOT ALL GLADIATOR FIGHTS ENDED IN DEATH THOUGH — IT'S THOUGHT THAT ONLY ONE IN FIVE BOUTS ENDED THIS WAY.

THE EMPEROR'S DUNGEON
CARCERE MAMERTINO

This was Ancient Rome's maximum security prison. There was an upper level and a lower dungeon, the *Tullianum*, where luckless prisoners were thrown into the damp darkness, sometimes to be killed. The Christian apostle Peter was said to have performed a miracle while locked up here. The story goes that he hit the rock and made water gush out, using it to baptise other prisoners.

LUDUS MAGNUS

CARCERE MAMERTINO

BULGE BELOW
PANTHEON FLOOR

Everyone looks up at the famous dome of the Pantheon building (see page 92) but if you look down at the marble floor you'll see that it's slightly convex (it bulges up in the middle). This allows rain to drain away through drainage holes around the edge. Rain comes into the building through the *oculus* (the hole in the top of the dome), which was added by the Ancient Romans as a door between the humans below and the gods above.

ENTER ANCIENT ROME
PALAZZO VALENTINI

The underground ruins of two well-to-do villas, still with their floor mosaics, were found here. Now, with the help of a light and sound show, visitors can see the rooms recreated before their eyes, meet the people who once lived there and even see ancient rain falling on a Roman garden. There's a tragedy hidden here, though. One of the biggest rooms has a shattered mosaic with burn marks on it, and archaeologists think this might have happened when a fire ripped through the home.

PALAZZO VALENTINI

PANTHEON

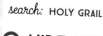search: HOLY GRAIL

HIDE AND SEEK

According to legend, Pope Sixtus II didn't want Emperor Valerian getting his hands on the Holy Grail (a very special cup linked to Jesus) so he gave it to St. Lawrence to hide in a safe place. Some people believe the Holy Grail is hidden near St. Lawrence's tomb in Rome.

STAMP OF THE CITY

MANHOLE COVERS

All Rome's manhole covers are stamped S.P.Q.R. It stands for *Senatus Populusque Romanus*, meaning 'The Senate and People of Rome'. You'll see the letters on the *nasoni* fountains, too (see page 18). The letters were used in Ancient Roman times and once appeared on the battle flags of the Roman army.

WHAT'S THAT DOWN THERE?

RIVER TIBER

Tourists sometimes get a big surprise when they're looking down at the River Tiber from one of Rome's bridges. They suddenly see weird swimming creatures that look like giant rats crossed with beavers! They're coypus, originally from South America. They were brought over to Italy to be farmed for their fur and meat, but some escaped and now coypus live wild in the city's river.

ALL OVER ROME

RIVER TIBER

GOING GRUESOME

Like all cities, Rome has its grisly side. Prepare yourself to enter the creepiest corners of town and encounter mummies, body parts, scary pictures and even a mysterious stone with the devil's claw mark on it. Then settle in for a bloodcurdling gladiator show... if you dare!

MIXED-UP MUMMIES

GREGORIAN EGYPTIAN MUSEUM

There are nine Ancient Egyptian mummies in the Vatican Museums, along with 18 mummified body parts. But it turns out that some of them are fakes. Scientists using the latest technology discovered that two of the smallest mummies had authentic mummy bandages but the bones came from centuries later. One of them even contained an iron nail from the 1800s.

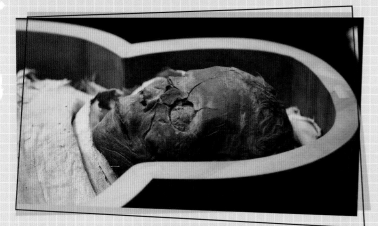

MUSEUM OF WICKEDNESS

CRIME MUSEUM

This gruesome museum of Italian crime was once used to teach prison guards. Now its collection of murder weapons, punishment equipment and real-life crime stories is open to the public. One of the grisliest items on display is the Milazzo Cage, a human-shaped cage once used to hang the remains of criminals outside for everyone to see. It was found in the wall of a Sicilian prison with a skeleton still inside it.

START

GREGORIAN EGYPTIAN MUSEUM

CRIME MUSEUM

search: SLAVERY IN ANCIENT TIMES

📍 IT'S A SLAVE'S LIFE

Ancient Roman slaves were very useful, so they rarely got the death penalty. Here are a few of the punishments they could receive:

- Being branded on the forehead or whipped
- Being made to carry a piece of wood around their neck
- Being sent to the workhouse to turn a mill to grind corn

STONE-PROOF SAINT

BASILICA DI SANTA SABINA

A mysterious shiny black stone, pockmarked with grooves and holes, sits on a column in this church. The marks are said to have been made by the claws of the devil himself! This tall tale of a forked tail tells how St. Dominic was busy praying at the church altar in 1220 when the devil arrived to tempt him. When Dominic ignored his fiery visitor the 'Lord of Hell' lost his cool, ripped a stone from the roof and hurled it, only to see it bounce harmlessly off the holy man.

"I didn't feel a thing!"

CLIFF COMEUPPANCE

TARPEIAN ROCK

This cliff on the Capitoline Hill was the spot where murderers and traitors were pushed to their deaths in Ancient Roman times. The story goes that during the ancient Sabine Wars (wars between Rome and a neighbouring tribe), a woman called Tarpeia betrayed the Romans. She agreed to unlock a gate and let the Sabines enter in return for what they wore on their left arms. She meant their gold bracelets, but once they were in they killed her by crushing her with the shields they carried on their left arms. Then they threw her over the cliff.

TARPEIAN ROCK

SCULPTURES WITH STORIES

CENTRALE MONTEMARTINI SCULPTURE MUSEUM

Ancient Roman art often has gruesome myths attached to it. For instance, this museum has a sculpture of poor old Marsyas, a mythical servant of the gods who thought he could play music better than the god Apollo. He made the mistake of challenging the god to a musical competition, lost and was killed – a tough way to lose a talent contest.

WALL OF NIGHTMARES

CHIESA DI SANTA STEFANO ROTONDO

There are 36 gruesome murals (wall paintings) in this otherwise lovely church. They were added in the 1500s and they show Christian martyrs dying in many horrible ways. The names of the emperors who ordered the awful deaths appear above each mural.

WHEN BRITISH AUTHOR CHARLES DICKENS VISITED THE MURALS IN THE 1800S HE WAS SHOCKED, AND WROTE: 'SUCH A PANORAMA OF HORROR AND BUTCHERY NO MAN COULD IMAGINE IN HIS SLEEP, THOUGH HE WERE TO EAT A WHOLE PIG RAW FOR SUPPER.'

DEAD DECOR
CONVENT OF THE CAPUCHINS

The Capuchin monks who lived in this
monastery from 1528 to 1870 decided
to remind themselves that life is fleeting.
They used the bones of around 4,000 dead
monks to decorate the church crypt as
a reminder of death to come. The bones
were used to make everything from picture
frames, wall decorations and archways to
light fittings. Mummified monks in robes
are hanging around, some of them acting
as wall lights.

**CONVENT OF
THE CAPUCHINS**

HOLY, NOT HORRIBLE
RELIGIOUS RELICS

Rome's churches contain many religious relics,
the supposed body parts of saints. They may
seem gruesome to non-Catholics, but Catholics
consider them holy. They're usually in elaborate
display cases in chapels off the main church.

ROME'S TOP RELICS

The bones of the
apostle **St. Peter**

The heads of the apostles
St. Peter and St. Paul

John the Baptist's head
(though it's one of four
claimed around the world)

St. Cecilia's bones
along with the supposed
remains of the bath in
which she was murdered

The finger of **St. Thomas.**
According to the Bible he
used it to touch the wound
of Jesus after Jesus rose
from the dead.

The head of **St. Valentine.**
On Valentine's Day you
can tour the catacombs
under the church where
his skull is kept.

☠ GAMES OF DEATH

THE COLOSSEUM

From AD 80 onwards the Colosseum was the place where Ancient Roman citizens could enjoy day after day of free games paid for by the emperor or by important senators. The games featured bloodthirsty fights to the death between gladiators, along with criminal executions and wild animal hunts.

THE COLOSSEUM

UP FOR GRABS

Wooden balls were sometimes thrown into the audience containing tokens for prizes, from money and food treats to properties in Rome. Crowd fights sometimes broke out as spectators tried to grab them.

FIGHT TO THE END

Gladiators were prisoners of war, slaves or people who were so in debt that they had to risk death to try to make money. If gladiators survived they became celebrities, gained their freedom and could retire wealthy. But if they died in the arena their bodies were dragged out on the end of a hook, through the 'Gate of Death'. If they weren't quite dead they were finished off with a mallet.

BEASTLY BEHAVIOUR

Thousands of animals died in the arena, too. Games organisers had exotic creatures shipped to Rome to please the crowds. Hippos, tigers, lions, giraffes and bears were among the creatures pushed out onto the arena floor, confused and scared, to be killed for entertainment. Afterwards their meat was sold by local butchers.

SEATS FOR SOME

VIPs had the most comfortable seats. Women and slaves had the worst, high up and crowded, with only a distant view of the action. Shade awnings were stretched over some seats on sweltering hot days, and sometimes the crowd got a free sprinkling of scented water.

80,000
MAXIMUM CAPACITY

80
THE NUMBER OF PUBLIC ENTRANCES. IT WAS RATHER LIKE A MODERN SPORTS STADIUM, WITH NUMBERED SEATS.

THE COLOSSEUM WAS BUILT USING SLAVE LABOUR, STONE AND A RECENTLY INVENTED WONDER MATERIAL – CONCRETE.

DIFFERENT BACK THEN

IT'S HARD FOR US TO GRASP THE SHEER BRUTALITY OF THE ANCIENT ROMAN GAMES, AND WHY PEOPLE ENJOYED THEM. WE CAN ONLY ASSUME THAT ANCIENT ROMANS THOUGHT VERY DIFFERENTLY FROM US. THEY PROBABLY SAW THE GAME DEATHS AS OFFERINGS TO THE GODS, AND THOUGHT THAT THIS KIND OF END WAS IN SOME WAY NOBLE. THEY DID NOT VALUE THE LIVES OF SLAVES OR PRISONERS OF WAR WHO WERE FORCED TO BECOME GLADIATORS.

UNDER THE STAGE

Down below the arena there were shadowy, sweltering cells where gladiators and condemned criminals waited their turn and wild animals were kept in cages. When it was time for them to appear, they were winched up through trapdoors by gangs of slaves hauling on ropes.

PARTY DAYS

Get ready for a party trail through Rome's calendar of unique celebrations, from confetti throwing and pillow fighting to miraculous snowfalls and a special day for pets. Oh, and there's no need to bring snacks for the trip because there's lots of delicious festival food on offer.

START

PIAZZA DEL POPOLO

OK! IT'S NEW YEAR!
CAVOUR BRIDGE DIVE

On 1 January every year, crowds gather to watch daredevil divers plunge 17m (55.7ft) into the freezing River Tiber from the Cavour Bridge. The brave divers launch themselves off the bridge at midday, as soon as nearby cannons fire. Between 1996 and 2015, the star of the show was a lifeguard nicknamed Mr OK. He retired in 2015 and was awarded a medal by the city's mayor, who declared him 'Guardian of the Tiber'.

CAVOUR BRIDGE

CARNIVAL TIME

PIAZZA DEL POPOLO

At Carnival time there's a city parade, and children come to the Piazza del Popolo in their best fancy dress to throw colourful confetti called *coriandoli* around. Carnival traditionally runs for ten days before Ash Wednesday, which marks the beginning of the Christian period of Lent in either February or March.

EVERYBODY MAKES SURE THEY GET THEIR SHARE OF CARNIVAL TREATS

~* FRAPPE *~
BOW-SHAPED FRITTERS

* CASTAGNOLE *
SUGAR-COATED FRIED DOUGH BALLS

BEST DAY FOR BIG SOFTIES

PILLOW FIGHT, PIAZZA SANTA MARIA

At the end of April, a flash mob arrives in this square carrying pillows. Some of them wear pyjamas and slippers. When the local church bells ring at 6pm they launch into a mass pillow fight for International Pillow Fight Day. It's been taking place since 2006 in cities around the world, and Romans love it!

LARGO DI TORRE ARGENTINA

ASSASSINATION ACT

LARGO DI TORRE ARGENTINA

In 44 BC, Roman leader Julius Caesar was murdered in this exact spot by senators outside a political meeting hall. Every year members of a historical society dress up and re-enact the death, which took place on the 'Ides of March' (15 March). Caesar's attackers included his one-time friend Brutus, who might even have been his son. His famous last words were reported to be: *'Tu quoque, Brute, fili mi!'* ('You too, Brutus, my son!').

CIRCUS MAXIMUS

HAPPY BIRTHDAY

NATALE DI ROMA, MAINLY
CAMPIDOGLIO & CIRCUS MAXIMUS

Gladiators and Roman soldiers are out and about on 21 April, parading through town to celebrate Rome's birthday. According to tradition, the city was founded in 753 BC (see page 10 for the full story), which means it's had a lot of birthday parties!

EVERY YEAR, A TRENCH-DIGGING CEREMONY RE-ENACTS AN EVENT FROM WHEN ROME WAS FOUNDED. A HOLE WAS DUG AND OFFERINGS OF THE FIRST FRUITS OF THE SEASON WERE THROWN IN TO PERSUADE THE GODS TO BE KIND TO THE CITY'S INHABITANTS.

SUMMER SNOWFLAKES

FESTIVAL OF OUR LADY
OF THE SNOWS, BASILICA
DI SANTA MARIA MAGGIORE

On 5 August, at the height of Rome's hot summer, snowflakes fall at this church. Actually they're white rose petals representing the legend of a miraculous snow that was said to have fallen here in AD 352, creating the shape of the church floorplan on the ground. It was considered a holy sign from the Virgin Mary to build the church on this spot.

BASILICA DI SANTA
MARIA MAGGIORE

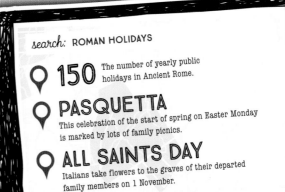

150 The number of yearly public holidays in Ancient Rome.

PASQUETTA
This celebration of the start of spring on Easter Monday is marked by lots of family picnics.

ALL SAINTS DAY
Italians take flowers to the graves of their departed family members on 1 November.

CHIESA DI SANT'EUSEBIO

ALL OVER ROME

BLESSING OF THE BEASTS

PET BLESSING, CHIESA DI SANT'EUSEBIO

The Catholic feast day of St. Antony the Abbot, patron saint of animals, is on 17 January. It's the day when locals can take their pets to be blessed in this church. Cats, dogs and birds all sit listening to the priest's sermon and then their owners take them outside to be blessed one by one. If pets can't attend, it's OK to bring a photo.

FESTIVAL FOOD

AROUND TOWN

Local districts of Rome have their own festivals, with special food as well as parties. At the Festival of San Guiseppe on 19 March the locals stock up on little custard-filled puffs called *bignè di San Giuseppe*. On 23 June everyone tucks into *lumache in umido* – stewed snails – at the Festival of San Giovanni. At Easter many inhabitants around town have a celebration picnic with some *torta pasqualina* – a delicious cheesy egg pie.

TAKE THE STAGE

Rome has been playing host to theatre, music and poetry for longer than just about anywhere in the world, and nowadays it's a movie-making city, too. Lights! Camera! Action! Choose a location for your starring role.

START

AUDITORIUM PARCO DELLA MUSICA

SOUNDS GOOD

AUDITORIUM PARCO DELLA MUSICA

These three giant pods are sometimes nicknamed beetles, turtles or computer mice. In fact, they are concert halls that play host to over 2 million visitors a year, making the site one of the biggest concert venues in the world. Their shape makes the acoustics (sound quality) great inside. The architect Renzo Piano bounced lasers off the walls to measure exactly how sound waves would behave. He also designed internal ceilings and walls so they could be moved to create different acoustics for different performers.

HIP HOP ROME

MUSIC FESTIVAL

Hip hop and rap are both popular in Rome. Every year there's a big international hip hop festival and DJ crews from around the world come to perform. You can also kick back, relax and watch breakdancing during the festival, too.

ALL AROUND ROME

search: ROMAN MOVIES

MOUTH OF TRUTH

In the film *Roman Holiday* a princess escapes her royal duties to wander around Rome. One of the places she visits is the Mouth of Truth. See page 27 for the legend surrounding this famous landmark. The princess didn't lose any of her fingers, but will you?

BAD PUPPET

TEATRINO DI PULCINELLA GIANICOLO

Every weekend, the Italian puppet Pulcinella and a cast of other well-known characters perform here. Pulcinella first appeared over 200 years ago. His name means 'little chicken', but in other countries he has become known as 'Punch'. In Italy, he has a famously beaky nose, a squeaky voice, a white costume and a black mask. He's greedy, crafty and bad-tempered, and he's prone to eating macaroni or hitting the other puppets with a wooden spoon!

LUNGOTEVERE

SUPER-FAST STEPS

LUNGOTEVERE

The James Bond film *Spectre* featured an incredible car chase down 68 steps and along this narrow walkway alongside the River Tiber. The 400-man film crew, plus safety frogmen waiting in the river, watched as stuntmen accelerated over and over again down the steps in an Aston Martin DB10 and a Jaguar C-X75, until the crew finally got all the shots they needed. Before the day of the shoot, the risky car moves had been rehearsed for three weeks at a disused airfield near Rome.

TEATRINO DI PULCINELLA GIANICOLO

NIGHT AT THE OPERA

BASILICA DI SANT'ANDREA DELLA VALLE

This beautiful church was a setting in one of the world's most famous operas, *Tosca* by Puccini, which takes place around Rome. Opera lovers can be found here, listening to the music on their headphones as they soak up the atmosphere.

Tosca was first performed in 1900, in Rome. It's a tale of love, trickery, politics and murder. The politics upset some people, and before the opening night there were threats of violence. When the curtain went up, the audience were heard shouting, and the scared composer thought things were going to get nasty. But he needn't have worried. People were shouting at annoying late arrivals.

THEATRE OF MARCELLUS

"Aaaargh! Urghhhh!"

BASILICA DI SANT'ANDREA DELLA VALLE

DEAD GOOD PERFORMANCES

THEATRE OF MARCELLUS

Two thousand years ago, Ancient Roman audiences of up to 11,000 people came here to see plays. These performances weren't like modern theatre shows. Actors wore costumes and masks to represent their characters, and two actors may have played each character – one reading the lines and one acting out the words. The plays were either comedies or tragedies, and occasionally real-life condemned criminals were killed onstage as part of the action.

Roman actors wore colour-coded clothes:

Rich man	Poor man	Slave	Woman	A god

STAGED DRAMA

THEATRE AT OSTIA ANTICA

This Ancient Roman theatre once had room for 4,000 spectators, and it is famous for the giant stone theatre masks that once decorated the building. Each character wore a smiling, leering, sad or angry mask and a colour-coded costume that the audience would recognise. Male characters wore brown masks and female characters wore white ones (though women were not allowed to act and men took their parts). The masks amplified the actors' voices, and the expressions were exaggerated so that everybody in the audience could see them.

CAMERAS ROLL IN ROME

CINECITTÀ STUDIOS

Over 3,000 movies have been made here, in the largest film studio in Europe. Children can sometimes take part in workshops, learning to make latex special-effects masks and exploring inside a mocked-up submarine once used in a movie. Films and TV shows set in Ancient Rome are often filmed here, such as classic movie *Ben Hur* and an episode of *Doctor Who* that needed to recreate Pompeii as it looked 2,000 years ago, just before Mount Vesuvius erupted.

300 THE NUMBER OF DRESSING ROOMS FOR PERFORMERS

THE NUMBER OF STAGES **22**

CINECITTÀ STUDIOS

I'M IN CHARGE!

Rome is Italy's capital city and has always been at the centre of world history, so it's not surprising that its many rulers have left their mark around town. Follow in their footsteps and rule Rome your way by taking the trail of power and uncovering some of the secrets of the VIPs.

WALLS FOR WORRIED ROMANS

MUSEUM OF THE WALLS

In the third century AD, these huge Ancient Roman walls were built around the city and dotted with watchtowers to try to keep out barbarians threatening to invade from northern Europe. In the end it didn't work. In AD 410 Rome was attacked by Visigoths from the area we now call Germany. There were 16 gates around the walls, and one of the gates was opened, probably by rebellious slaves. The Visigoths, led by King Alaric, poured in and took control, taking all the valuables they could find.

19KM (12 MILES)
TOTAL LENGTH OF THE WALLS

380
NUMBER OF WATCHTOWERS ON THE WALLS

HOUSE IN A HOLE

GOLDEN HOUSE

Between AD 65 and 68 Roman emperor Nero built a huge palace for himself, nicknamed the Golden House because it was decorated with the finest marble, gemstones and a solid gold wall cladding. Just as the builders finished, Nero was overthrown and condemned to death, but he killed himself before he was caught by his enemies. In the 1400s a local fell down a hole and was amazed to find himself in a cave with beautifully painted walls. He had accidentally rediscovered the remains of the Golden House.

IN 2009, ARCHAEOLOGISTS DISCOVERED THE REVOLVING DINING ROOM IN THE GOLDEN HOUSE. HERE NERO'S GUESTS SAT FEASTING WHILE SLOWLY TURNING AROUND AND BEING SPRINKLED FROM ABOVE WITH PETALS AND PERFUME.

START

MUSEUM OF THE WALLS

GOLDEN HOUSE

search: WERE ROMAN EMPERORS NICE?

EMPERORS' TEMPERS

Peaceful – Rome was stable while Augustus was in charge.
Arrogant – Caligula insisted on being treated like a god!
Ruthless – Claudius had his wife killed.
Bullying – When blamed for the Great Fire of Rome,
Nero pointed the finger at the Christians.
Protective – Hadrian reduced the size of the
Roman Empire and built walls to protect it.

SPOT THE POPE'S KEYS
VARIOUS LOCATIONS

For centuries popes have ruled the Catholic Church from Rome.
They often commissioned buildings and fountains around town
and left their symbol on the design to make sure everyone
knew how generous they had been. Look out for badges that
incorporate two big keys and a headdress of three crowns.
The keys symbolise the keys to the kingdom of heaven, and
the headdress was once worn by popes. You can see one on
top of the Trevi Fountain on page 20.

**ARCH OF
SEPTIMIUS SEVERUS**

CARVING CRIME
**ARCH OF
SEPTIMIUS SEVERUS**

Originally this big triumphal arch
was dedicated to the Ancient Roman
emperor Severus and his two sons,
Geta and Caracalla. When Severus
died, Caracalla murdered his
brother and took control. He had
all mention of his brother taken
off the carvings on the arch, as
if Geta never existed, but it's
possible to see where the name
was chiselled away. His crime
can't be hidden, even after
nearly 2,000 years!

MURDER SCENE DISCOVERED

LARGO DI TORRE ARGENTINA

We know that Julius Caesar was killed here (see page 7), but where exactly? In 2012, the exact crime spot was rediscovered when archaeologists unearthed a big wide platform. We know from Roman writings that it was erected on the spot soon after the murder, to mark the deadly attack.

(see page 7)

LARGO DI TORRE
ARGENTINA

PRESIDENT'S PLACE

QUIRINALE PALACE

The President of Italy is based in this grand palace, filled with sumptuous decoration, art and tapestries. Visiting VIPs from around the world are entertained at grand palace banquets here. One of the palace's most unusual treasures is the water organ in the palace garden. Its keyboard is powered by a waterfall.

THE ELITE TROOPS OF THE PRESIDENTIAL HONOUR GUARD, THE *CORAZZIERI*, ARE TO BE SEEN HERE ON GRAND OCCASIONS. THEY WEAR IMPRESSIVE UNIFORMS AND HELMETS WITH BIG HORSEHAIR PLUMES ON TOP.

FAMILY FOUNTAIN

FOUNTAIN OF THE BEES

Many popes came from wealthy families who lived in their own palaces. Just as popes left their symbols around town, so did Rome's VIP families. You can spot their coats of arms all over the city. The Barberini family had bees on their coat of arms, and water comes out of the mouths of Barberini bees on this fountain. It could have been different – the Barberinis once had horse flies as their symbol but they changed it to something sweeter!

Here are some of the other **VIP** family crests to be found around Rome.

Farnese family   Pamphili family   Chigi family   Colonna family

FIRST FAMILY

ROMAN PEACE ALTAR

The Ancient Roman emperor Augustus had this giant altar carved to make animal sacrifices to the gods. It shows a grand religious procession, with everybody wearing their best robes, and it's now protected inside a giant glass box in the middle of Rome. It's unusual because it shows the emperor's whole family, including his stepchildren, nieces and nephews. They may look cute on the carving, but some of them would later kill each other in their struggle for power.

CASTLE TIMES

CASTEL SANT'ANGELO

Rome has its own guardian angel, towering above the city on top of an old castle with a secret passageway. Explore Castel Sant'Angelo in the footsteps of attackers, defenders and unlucky prisoners.

CASTEL SANT'ANGELO

TOP TOMB

The castle site began as a giant Ancient Roman tomb. The emperor Hadrian had his mausoleum (tomb) built here, ready for his own death. Later other emperors' bodies were also placed here, and the castle was eventually built on top. Visitors enter the castle through Hadrian's tomb room, but there are no remains. They were scattered long ago by invaders.

THE ANGEL ARRIVES

The castle got its name in AD 590 when Pope St. Gregory is said to have had a vision of the angel St. Michael on top of the castle walls. He was predicting the end of a plague that had swept through the city. The giant bronze statue of St. Michael on the top of the castle looks like he's going to leap off and fly across Rome.

HADRIAN THE HIPSTER

A statue of Hadrian in a chariot once stood on top of the site. He was the first Roman emperor to grow a beard, and he started a fashion. When people around the Roman Empire saw his bearded face on coins, they copied him and began growing trendy beards, too.

XVIII

ARMOUR INSIDE

The castle now houses a museum of arms and armour, including a giant wooden crossbow that fired javelins and an ancient helmet used by an Etruscan gladiator around 2,500 years ago. In the castle courtyard there are stacks of marble cannonballs ready to fire at enemies.

PAPAL ESCAPE ROUTE

The castle became the Pope's private stronghold, and there's a hidden passageway from the Vatican to the castle, called the *passetto*. In 1494, Pope Alexander VI ran through it to escape the invading troops of Charles VII, and the story goes that the soldiers shot at his white robes as he ran for his life.

THE *PASSETTO* IS HIDDEN INSIDE THIS OLD FORTIFIED WALL

16 YEARS THE NUMBER OF YEARS IT TOOK TO BUILD THE CASTLE

48M HIGH (157 FEET) THE HEIGHT OF CASTEL SANT'ANGELO

5 THE NUMBER OF FLOORS

IN HOT WATER!

IN 1527, ROME WAS ATTACKED AND POPE CLEMENT VII ESCAPED TO THE SAFETY OF THE CASTLE VIA THE *PASSETTO*. EVENTUALLY HE HAD TO SURRENDER AND WAS LOCKED UP IN THE CASTLE, BUT HE BRIBED GUARDS AND ESCAPED DISGUISED AS A PEDLAR (SOMEONE WHO SOLD THINGS ON THE STREET). LIFE WASN'T TOO TOUGH FOR HIM IN THE CASTLE, THOUGH — HE HAD A LUXURY BATHROOM, SAID TO BE THE FIRST RUNNING HOT AND COLD WATER BATHROOM IN THE WORLD!

MEET THE CREATURES

Rome is full of creatures, both real and mythical. Get ready to meet a wolf, a treasure cat, some strange door monsters, a rude stone elephant and some of the real animals that have made Rome their home.

MUM'S YOUNGER THAN SHE LOOKS

START

CAPITOLINE WOLF

Rome's founders, Romulus and Remus, are said to have been rescued as babies by a she-wolf (find out more about the legend on page 10). A statue of the wolf stood in Ancient Rome, and for many years this famous bronze statue was thought to be the original. Modern science spoilt things when it was recently dated to medieval times.

CAPITOLINE WOLF

"Dinner time, boys!"

HELPING THE HOMELESS

ROME'S CATS

Rome has many stray cats, and the city now has a couple of sanctuaries where they are fed and medically treated. There's one in the Largo di Torre Argentina (Caesar's murder spot), and one in the cemetery near the Pyramid of Cestius, where cats pad around the famous tombs of Romantic poets Keats and Shelley.

ALL OVER ROME

PERHAPS IT'S NOT SURPRISING THAT THERE ARE SO MANY CATS IN ROME. THEY'VE BEEN IN THE CITY SINCE ANCIENT ROMAN TIMES, WHEN THEY WERE BROUGHT IN FROM EGYPT. CATS WERE SACRED IN ANCIENT EGYPT AND IT WAS ILLEGAL FOR THEM TO LEAVE, SO THEY WERE SMUGGLED OUT BY CAT-NAPPERS.

ELEFANTINO

ELE-INSULT

ELEFANTINO

This stone elephant was carved in the 1600s to carry an Ancient Egyptian obelisk that had been found in the garden of a monastery. The resident priest did not like its design and insisted that a big cube was added under the elephant's belly, which made the elephant look extra fat. The designer, Bernini, was ordered to make the change, but as an insult to the priest he positioned the elephant with its backside facing the monastery!

TREASURE CAT

VIA DELLA GATTA (STREET OF THE CAT)

A small marble cat looks out from the corner of the Palazzo Grazioli and gives this street its name. It probably came from the Ancient Roman Temple of Isis, where cats would have been considered sacred. Legend has it that the cat is looking towards a place where a great treasure is hidden, but though many have tried to follow its gaze, no riches have ever turned up.

VIA DELLA GATTA

CHARGE!

SIENA SQUARE

Rome's International Horse Show takes place in spring, and is famous for its finale, when 145 *carabinieri* (military police) re-enact a charge from the Battle of Pastrengo in 1848. Half of the horses taking part are grey and the other half are chestnut-coloured. They step together perfectly side by side and charge in perfect unison. Some bow to the audience and some even play dead after the mock battle.

SIENA SQUARE

MONSTERS LIVE HERE

PALAZZO ZUCCARI

The architect and painter Federico Zuccari decided to build a house that was a little different. The door and windows that led to his garden were surrounded by giant gaping monster masks called *mascherone*. His plans turned out to be monstrous for Zuccari. The building of the house nearly ruined him financially.

ANCIENT PETS

Ancient Rome is thought to be one of the first civilisations to introduce dogs as pets.

Ancient Roman men used bigger breeds of dogs for hunting and the smaller breeds were companions for women.

Ancient Roman cats were kept to keep away rodents.

ROMAN SKIES

AERIAL SHOW
LOOK TO THE SKIES

About a million starlings migrate across northern Europe in the autumn, and when they reach Rome they create amazing swirling patterns in the sky, called murmurations, as they swoop and rise together in flocks. Their droppings are a problem, but the locals love their sky shows, which usually take place at dusk when the birds are about to settle for the night.

BIOPARCO DI ROMA

COOL FOR CREATURES
ZOO, BIOPARCO DI ROMA

When temperatures soar in the summer it can get very hot for the animals at Rome's zoo, so they're given special treats to cool them down. The big cats get ice cubes with meat inside. The monkeys get bamboo canes to suck, filled with frozen yoghurt and watermelon. Fruit ice lollies are given to many of the animals to lick, and even the hippos get cooling, juicy watermelons to munch!

THE HOLY WAY

Rome is the home of the Catholic Church, which has its own country – Vatican City – in the heart of Rome. Discover some unusual facts about the basilicas (churches) around town and then follow the crowds to Vatican City and St. Peter's Basilica.

CHRISTMAS TREAT

BASILICA DEI SANTI COSMA E DAMIANO

This church is built into the back of the Roman Forum (see pages 6-11). Every Christmas, crowds come to see its beautiful detailed *presepio* (nativity scene), which was made in the 1700s. There are hundreds of little animals and people in the scene, set among mini Roman ruins. Carved or pottery nativity scenes like this are traditionally made in Naples and are still produced there today.

THE BASILICA OF ST. JOHN LATERAN WAS REPUTEDLY WHERE A TERRIBLE EVENT TOOK PLACE IN 897. THE STORY GOES THAT GOD WAS SO ANGRY WHEN THE DEAD BODY OF POPE FORMOSUS WAS DUG UP AND PUT ON TRIAL THAT HE SENT AN EARTHQUAKE AND A FIRE THAT NEARLY DESTROYED THE BUILDING.

SWEATING CENOTAPH

BASILICA OF ST. JOHN LATERAN

This is one of Rome's oldest churches and one of its features is Pope Sylvester II's cenotaph (funeral monument). According to legend, if the monument feels damp it's a sign that a cardinal or a bishop will soon die. If it starts to sweat beads of water, the pope will be the one to go. Sylvester II was pope 1,000 years ago. A scholar who studied maths and astronomy, he was accused by his enemies of being a sorcerer in league with the devil.

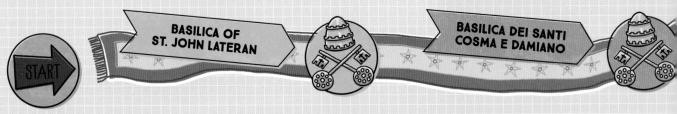

START

BASILICA OF ST. JOHN LATERAN

BASILICA DEI SANTI COSMA E DAMIANO

FANTASTIC FAKE

ST. IGNATIUS CHURCH

There's a fabulous fake dome painted on the ceiling of this church. Apparently the church ran out of money to build a proper dome and so ordered a painted one instead. Artist Andrea Pozzo painted the convincing curved-looking ceiling on a completely flat surface. Not only is the dome shape fake, the painting is a fake, too. Pozzo's masterpiece was destroyed by fire and repainted in 1823 based on his drawings.

ST. PETER IN
CHAINS CHURCH

STATUE SLIP

ST. PETER IN CHAINS CHURCH

World-renowned artist Michelangelo provided the statue of Moses for a pope's tomb in this church. Moses is 2.4m (8ft) high, even sitting down. He's got big muscly arms, a long beard and a stern face. But the most surprising thing about him is that he has two horns on his head. This apparently comes from a mistranslation of Hebrew words in the Old Testament. The original Hebrew described rays of light coming from Moses' head, but it was translated as horns.

search: VATICAN FACTS

ONLINE

Keep up with Vatican life by looking at its live webcams or join around 7 million others by following the Pope on Twitter. His tweets are translated into nine languages, including Latin.

BIRD LIFE

The Vatican is home to some wild monk parrots. Peregrine falcons also nest there and have been seen swooping down on the pigeons in St. Peter's Square.

SAINT AGNES'S SPOT

CHIESA DI SANT'AGNESE IN AGONE

This church, on Piazza Navona, is said to stand on the site of a miracle performed by St. Agnes. She lived in Ancient Roman times and was punished for being Christian. As a public humiliation she was made to stand here naked, but the story goes that her hair instantly grew very long and covered her up. An angel came to guard over her, too. A relic said to be her skull is displayed inside the church.

BASILICA DI SANTA
MARIA IN TRASTEVERE

CHIESA DI
SANT'AGNESE IN AGONE

MIRACLES
AND MARTYRS

BASILICA DI SANTA
MARIA IN TRASTEVERE

According to legend, this church stands on the place where a spring of pure oil suddenly came out of the ground on the day that Jesus was born. A column next to the altar marks the exact spot where the miracle occurred. One of the church's other treasures is the head of St. Apollonia, a Christian martyr who lost her life in Ancient Roman times. She had all her teeth pulled out by her enemies, so she was later chosen to be the patron saint of dentists.

WORLD'S SMALLEST COUNTRY

THE VATICAN

The world's smallest state takes up 0.44 sq km (0.169 sq miles) of Rome. It has its own Head of State (the Pope), language (Latin) and army (the Swiss Guard). It issues its own coins and stamps, and even has its own radio station and TV studio. Around 450 people have citizenship, with their own Papal passports, though in all around 800 people live in the city. Only people appointed by the Catholic Church can become citizens.

✝ The Vatican has its own car number plate letters – SVC or CV.

✝ Citizens of the Vatican don't pay any tax. State services are funded by museum entrance fees, stamp and souvenir sales.

✝ Vatican coins can be spent wherever euros are accepted.

✝ The Vatican's flag is yellow and white. It shows the keys to heaven and the Pope's three-crowned hat. The gold key represents heavenly power. The silver key represents power on Earth, and the two are joined together with a red cord.

ST. PETER'S SQUARE

St. Peter's Square lies in front of St. Peter's Basilica, the pope's church. Once someone walks into the square they have left Italy and are in the Vatican State, but they don't have to go through passport control. Crowds gather to hear the pope when he speaks from his balcony. Columns around the square symbolise arms welcoming people to the church. In the middle there's an obelisk from Ancient Egypt, which acts as a giant sundial.

ST. PETER'S SQUARE

320M X 240M (1,050FT X 787FT) = THAT'S ROUGHLY **THE SIZE OF 7 FOOTBALL PITCHES** X7

284 COLUMNS

140 THE NUMBER OF SAINT STATUES ABOVE THE COLUMNS

THE VATICAN

THE GREAT CHURCH

ST PETER'S, THE VATICAN

Millions of people visit St. Peter's Basilica, one of the world's biggest churches, and the Vatican palaces, which are home to lots of Vatican museums. The basilica was first built in the 300s over the spot where the apostle St. Peter was said to have been buried.

6.4KM (4 MILES) OF GALLERIES AND GARDENS

6 MILLION VISITORS EACH YEAR

70,000 WORKS OF ART AND OBJECTS ON DISPLAY

THE POPE'S PLACE

Inside the church, the high altar is built on what is said to be St. Peter's tomb. Only the pope can celebrate Mass (the main Catholic religious ceremony) at the altar, which is covered in a 29m (95ft) ceremonial canopy called a baldachin.

ST. PETER'S BASILICA

THE BASILICA WE SEE NOW TOOK 120 YEARS TO BUILD. IT WAS FINISHED IN 1626.

ST PETER'S BASILICA

OPENING UP

Every morning at 5:45 a.m., five officials begin unlocking the 300 rooms that make up the Vatican's museums. There are 2,797 Vatican keys in all, and the doors are all numbered. Five more officials lock up everything at the end of the day. The key to the Sistine Chapel is put into a sealed envelope every night.

SISTINE CHAPEL

EGYPTIAN OBELISK

SACRED SCULPTURES

A famous statue called the Pietà stands inside the church. It shows the Virgin Mary holding the body of Christ, and was sculpted by Michelangelo. It's the only sculpture he ever signed, carving his name on Mary's sash. The Pietà is now kept behind bulletproof glass, after it was attacked with a hammer in the 1970s.

MICHELANGELO'S SIGNATURE

FLAT FEET!

There's also a famous 13th-century statue of St. Peter. Its feet have been worn away by centuries of pilgrims kissing and stroking them.

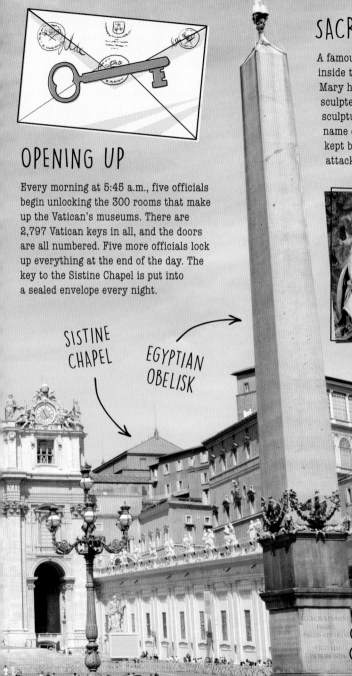

POPE'S GUARD

THE SWISS GUARD IS RESPONSIBLE FOR THE POPE'S SAFETY. READ ABOUT THEIR UNIFORM ON PAGE 70. WHEN THE GUARD WAS FIRST FOUNDED IN 1506, SWISS SOLDIERS WERE THOUGHT TO MAKE THE BEST AND MOST LOYAL MERCENARIES (PAID FOREIGN TROOPS) IN THE WORLD. EVEN NOW, THE GUARD IS MADE UP OF 100% SWISS CITIZENS. THESE HIGHLY TRAINED MARKSMEN ALSO LEARN TO USE THEIR SWORDS AND HALBERDS (THE AXE-LIKE LONG WEAPONS THEY HOLD ON PARADE).

WEAR ROME

La Bella Figura is an important expression in Italy. It means looking one's best, and it's why so many Italian people dress so well at all times! La Bella Figura is on display everywhere in Rome, from fashionable shops to smart uniforms. Take a style trip through town to see who's wearing what.

START

CENTRAL ROME

DESIGNER POLICE
REPUBLIC DAY PARADE

On 2 June there's a big parade in Rome to celebrate Italy's Republic Day. Lots of different Italian military uniforms are on show, including the Italian military police, the *carabinieri*. Their modern black and blue uniforms, with red stripes on the trousers, are created by the Italian fashion designer, Valentino. On special occasions they wear bicorne (two-pointed) hats with big feather plumes on top.

ELEGANCE EVERYWHERE
DECORATIVE ARTS MUSEUM

Budding fashionistas will love this collection of elegant clothes from the 1900s, featuring many top Italian fashion designers. There are around 800 outfits and accessories to see, many from the early 1900s, when Rome's best-dressed ladies were wearing the very finest gowns around.

DECORATIVE ARTS MUSEUM

FASHION CENTRAL
VIA DEI CONDOTTI

The world's top fashion houses have their shops on this street, where celebrities are sometimes to be seen buying their clothes, diamonds and bags. Actors Pierce Brosnan and Daniel Craig got suits made for their James Bond movies at Brioni, known for being one of the best tailors on the planet.

VIA DEI CESTARI

VIA DEI CONDOTTI

ROADS OF ROBES
VIA DEI CESTARI, VIA DI SANTA CHIARA

Shops in these two streets sell everything that Catholic priests need, from robes, shoes and hats to all sorts of religious accessories. This is the home of Annibale Gammarelli, the tailors who make the pope's white robes. When a new pope is about to be chosen, three sets of robes are made in three different sizes. That way a set is instantly ready for whoever gets the job, whatever their size.

Vatican wardrobe

The Pope wears a white cassock (robe), a short white cape called a *mozzetta* and a white skull cap called a *zucchetto*.

Cardinals wear red cassocks, *mozzettas* and red *birettas* (square caps with three points on top).

FEBRUARY FACES

CARNIVAL, PIAZZA NAVONA

At Carnival time in February (see page 44), fancy dress is everywhere, both in the Carnival parade and the watching crowds. Italian masquerade masks are often worn at this time. They were invented centuries ago as a disguise so that everyone could party together, whoever they were.

Traditional Italian party masks

Colombina
An elegant mask that covers half the face.

Volto
A mask that covers the whole face and makes a great disguise.

Medico della Peste
A mask used by plague doctors centuries ago. They stuffed herbs into the long beak to mask the smell of their patients.

SPECIAL SQUAD

SWISS GUARD

The Swiss Guard, the pope's private army of bodyguards, was founded over 500 years ago (find out more about them on page 67). Their ceremonial blue, red and yellow outfit, called the Gala Uniform, dates from those times.

The Swiss Guard also have everyday blue uniforms and ordinary business suits for blending into the crowd when they are guarding the pope on tour.

SWISS GUARDS' CLOTHES GIVE US A COOL VIEW OF THE PAST! AN ACCOUNT OF WHEN THEY FAMOUSLY FIRST ARRIVED IN ROME DOESN'T DESCRIBE THEM AS DIFFERENT FROM OTHER SOLDIERS' CLOTHES — BUT THE POPE WAS PAYING FOR THEM SO THEY WERE PROBABLY THE BEST!

search: COMPETITIVE CLOTHING

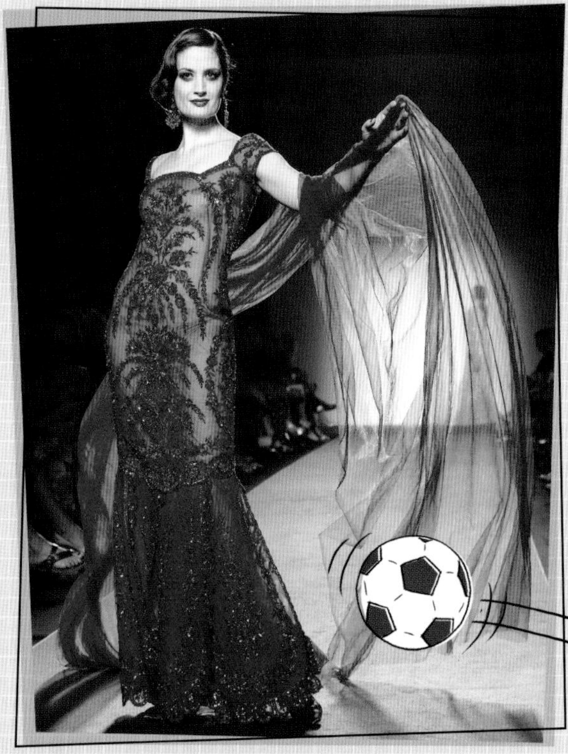

PRIZED POSSESSIONS

Altaroma – the Roman fashion house that runs Rome's Fashion Week – holds an annual award ceremony that introduces the best of Italian-born or Italian-educated fashion to the world!

RED AND YELLOW PRIDE

COLOURS OF ROME

Rome's official colours are gold/yellow and dark red, as shown on the city's flag and worn on the football shirts of city football team A.S. Roma.

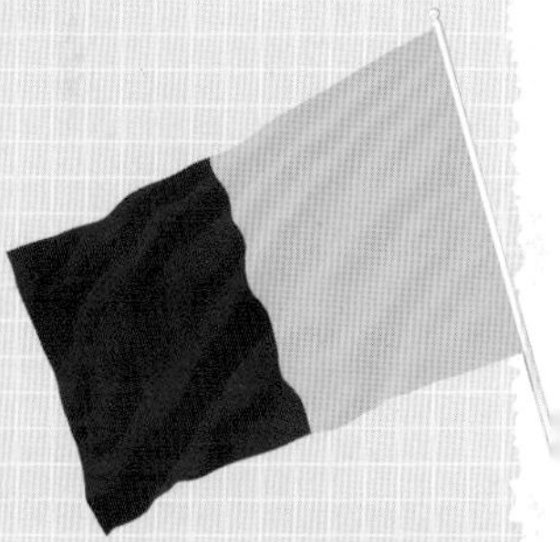

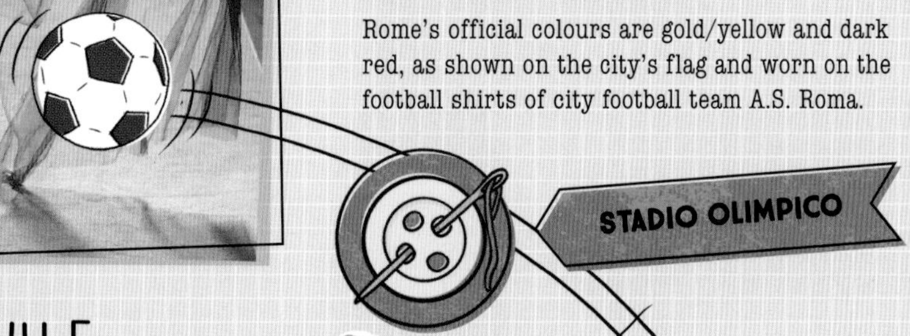

STADIO OLIMPICO

CITYWIDE STYLE

ALTAROMA

Every other year Rome holds Altaroma, a week of fashion celebrations with catwalk shows all around town. Italy has provided many of the world's best-known fashion designers, but Altaroma is also a chance for new designers to make a style splash by competing for the prestigious Talent Award.

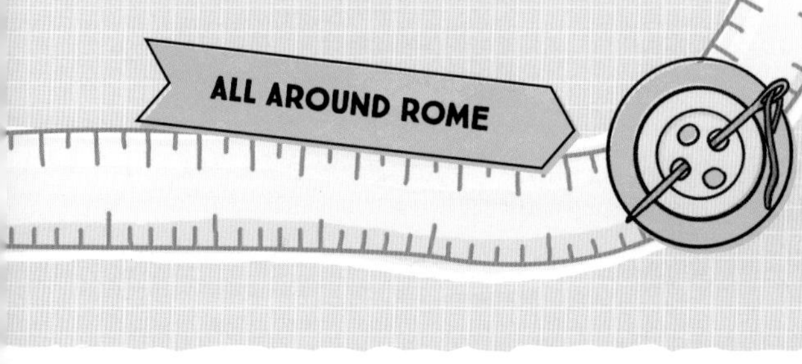

ALL AROUND ROME

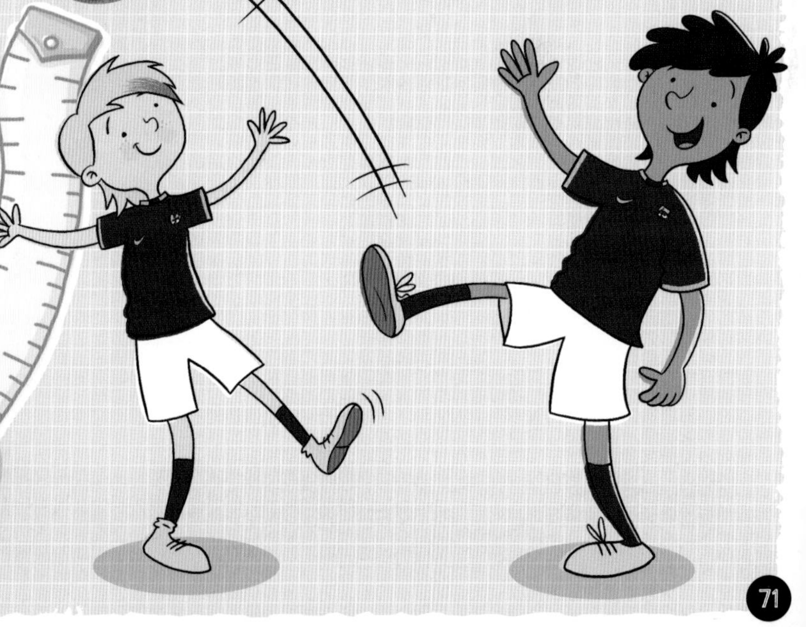

ANDIAMO!

How would you choose to get around Rome – a fast car, a Roman wagon, a train or perhaps even a strange flying machine? You'll need to be patient because Rome has had traffic jams since ancient times, but perhaps you'll be lucky and speed round with the help of a special saint. *Andiamo!* (Let's go!).

APPIAN WAY

ROMAN ROUTE
APPIAN WAY

The Appian Way is the famous Roman road that led from Rome all the way to Brindisi on the southeast coast of Italy. You can still walk along its original cobbles and see the remains of Ancient Roman VIP tombs that lined the route. (It was against the law for people to be buried in the city itself.) A wagon trip along the Appian Way could be dangerous though – bandit gangs lurked along some sections of the road.

POLICE WHEELS
MUSEUM OF POLICE CARS

Italian police cars and motorbikes from as far back as the 1930s are on display here, from neat little Fiats to grand stately old Alfa Romeos. Visitors can sometimes get to sit on a modern BMW police motorbike and pretend to be patrolling. These days some lucky Roman police officers get to drive Lamborghini Huracáns like the one pictured.

Police car nicknames:

PANTERA (panther)
A patrol car belonging to the State Police, or *Polizia*.

GAZELLA (gazelle)
A car driven by the Military Police, or *carabinieri*.

CIVETTA (owl)
An unmarked police car.

START

MUSEUM OF POLICE CARS

TWO WHEELS GOOD, FOUR WHEELS BAD

ALL OVER ROME

Scooters are found buzzing around the streets everywhere in Rome. The most famous brand is Vespa, known for its bright colours and cool style. The name Vespa was picked because it describes the buzzing noise the scooter makes. It's the Italian word for 'wasp'.

ALL OVER ROME

ROME HAS MORE **MOTORBIKES AND MOPEDS** THAN ANY OTHER **EUROPEAN CITY**

20-30% OF ROME'S TRAFFIC IS MADE UP OF **MOTORBIKES AND MOPEDS**

ST. FRANCESCA ROMANA CHURCH

BLESSED WHEELS

ST. FRANCESCA ROMANA CHURCH

This church houses the remains of St. Francesca Romana. Her skeleton lies inside, wearing a robe and holding a prayerbook. It was said that during her lifetime her path was always lit by an angel, which is why she was made the patron saint of motorists. On 9 March, her feast day, drivers bring their cars to the church to be blessed.

NEXT STOP, ANCIENT ROME

METRO LINE C

Work on Rome's new metro line has to stop every time the diggers unearth ancient ruins, which is tough on the builders because Rome is full of remains. In 2016, the railway workers unearthed the barracks of Emperor Hadrian's bodyguard along with 13 buried skeletons. The sleeping quarters, weapons rooms, kitchens and stables used by the bodyguards will now be put on show as part of a railway station. The line's due to be ready in 2021.

LEONARDO'S DRAWING OF A FLYING MACHINE SHOWS AN ENORMOUS PAIR OF WINGS ON A WOODEN FRAME. IT WOULD NEVER HAVE WORKED, BUT IT LOOKS A BIT LIKE A MODERN PARAGLIDER.

LEONARDO EXHIBITION

METRO LINE C

FIRST FLYING MACHINE

LEONARDO EXHIBITION

Leonardo da Vinci was born in Tuscany in 1452, and is known as one of the world's greatest artists. He was also an inventor, and more than 200 of his machine designs are on show here, along with working models and holograms created from his drawings. He came up with the idea of a flying machine, a tank and a diving suit 400 years or more before these things were actually created for real.

NUMBER ONE WHEELS

POPEMOBILES, THE VATICAN

The pope has his own cars, nicknamed Popemobiles, with the number plate SCV followed by a single number. SCV is short for the Latin *Status Civitatis Vaticanae*, which means Vatican City State. When the pope travels through a big crowd, he sometimes stands in a specially designed Popemobile with bulletproof glass sides, so that everyone can see him as he passes.

THE VATICAN

MILLE MIGLIA

search: ANCIENT RULES

📍 THE FIRST HIGHWAY CODE

Around 45 BC Julius Caesar brought in a new law banning wagons from entering Rome during the day, unless they were builders' wagons, dung carts or religious wheels. That meant most wagons came in at night, waking up Ancient Romans as they rumbled along the city cobbles.

ROME LOVES RACING

MILLE MIGLIA

The Ancient Romans were crazy about chariot racing and supported one of four city racing teams – the reds, whites, blues or greens. Rome hasn't lost its love of wheel racing and every year it hosts part of the Mille Miglia classic car race that runs from Rome to Brescia and back. Crowds come out to cheer on the cars, all of which date from between 1927 and 1957.

WIN HERE!

Put on your sports trainers and get ready to discover some of the city's best sporting action. World-class sports stars perform in Rome and it's no wonder that fans are so passionate about their favourites. People have been cheering winners here for thousands of years!

FRANCESCO TOTTI IS ROMA'S BEST-EVER PLAYER BY FAR, AND THE GOLDEN BOY OF 21ST-CENTURY ITALIAN SOCCER HE'S NICKNAMED *IL RE DI ROMA* (THE KING OF ROME).

FRANCESCO TOTTI

TEMPLE OF FOOTBALL

STADIO OLIMPICO

This 72,700-seat football stadium is home to Rome's two football teams, A.S. Roma and S.S. Lazio. Roma are nicknamed the *giallorossi* (the yellow and reds). Lazio are nicknamed the *biancazzuri* (the white and blues), after the club colours. Things can get smoky and noisy on the terraces here. Both sets of fans are known for smuggling in smoke flares and firecrackers, though these are banned.

SERVING UP SPORT

FORO ITALICO

Every year, part of this big sporting complex plays host to the world's top tennis players competing for millions in prize money. They play on clay courts to win the Italian Open, one of the tennis world's most important competitions. King of the Italian Open is Spanish star Rafael Nadal, who has won here seven times.

ROMA'S SHIRT BADGE SHOWS THE FAMOUS STATUE OF THE SHE-WOLF WITH ROME'S BABY FOUNDERS, ROMULUS AND REMUS (SEE PAGE 58).

LAZIO'S BADGE SHOWS A GOLDEN EAGLE, A SYMBOL OF ANCIENT ROME.

ROMA 1927

S.S. LAZIO

START
1 2 3
FORO ITALICO

STADIO OLIMPICO

ANCIENT HEROES

SPORTING STATUES, MUSEO NAZIONALE ROMANO

There are two very famous ancient sporting statues in this museum, both dug up in Rome in the 1800s. The marble Discus Thrower, which is also known as the *Lancellotti Discobolus*, is celebrated as one of the best-ever statues of an athlete. The bronze Boxer at Rest (also called the *Terme Boxer*) is very realistic. He looks exhausted after a fight and blood from his cuts is shown dripping down onto his body!

ICE IS NICE

WINTER ICE SKATING

The weather in Rome is rarely freezing, even in winter, but that doesn't stop people ice skating because rinks are set up around the city at Christmas time. There's usually a big one at the Auditorium Parco della Musica (see page 48). It does very occasionally snow in Rome, but only every 20 years or so. When it does everybody gets a big surprise!

ROME'S BIG RUN
ROME MARATHON

In springtime, the Rome Marathon takes place through the middle of town. Around 14,000 athletes set off from the Colosseum area to run past the cheering crowds. They're helped along by musicians and DJs performing at outdoor spots all along the course.

CELEBRITY RACERS

CIRCUS MAXIMUS

Once a Roman chariot track, the Circus Maximus now hosts big rock concerts and rallies. It once held 25,000 Ancient Romans cheering their favourite chariot drivers. The drivers were slaves and often died in nasty crashes. One of the most famous drivers of all, Scorpus, won over 2,000 races but was killed in AD 95. Drivers could earn big money. Celebrity charioteer Diocles is said to have earned the ancient equivalent of £12 billion by the time he retired in AD 146, making him the best-paid sportsman in the whole of world history!

CIRCUS MAXIMUS

> MOST RACES WERE BETWEEN CHARIOTS PULLED BY FOUR HORSES, BUT THERE WERE ALSO TWO-, SIX-, EIGHT- AND EVEN TEN-HORSE CHARIOT RACES.
> ACCIDENTS WERE CALLED *NAUFRAGIA* (SHIPWRECKS).
> DRIVERS WORE A SHORT TUNIC AND BODY PADDING, AND TIED THE HORSES' REINS ROUND THEIR WAIST. THEY HAD A CURVED KNIFE TO QUICKLY CUT THEMSELVES FREE IF THERE WAS AN ACCIDENT.
> THE WINNER WAS THE FIRST CHARIOT TO COMPLETE SEVEN LAPS.

POPULAR PASTIMES

- **Board games**
- **Hunting**
- **Watching gladiators fight** (very popular)
- **Paying for free gladiator fights for everyone** (emperors only!)

CLERICUS CUP
COLUMBUS PIUS XI FIELD

The Vatican has its own football world cup called the Clericus Cup, which is played between teams of priests and trainee priests from different countries. Instead of getting booked or sent off the field, they get 'sin-binned' and then forgiven. If they get shown a blue card for unsportsmanlike behaviour they have to go off the pitch for five minutes.

ROMAN RUGBY
ALL AROUND ROME

Rugby is a popular sport in Rome, and Italy is one the world's top international teams. It turns out that the Ancient Romans had a very similar game, called *harpastum*. Two teams passed a leather ball between them, trying to get it across a line, while stopping their opponents from doing the same. Ancient and modern Romans share a passion for ball games, especially team ones!

ALL AROUND ROME

GREEN ROME

Alongside all the fine marble historical buildings and statues, Rome also has lots of beautiful parks – sometimes called its 'green lungs'. The locals love to picnic in these parks at weekends and holiday times. Find out why by taking a stroll along the park path.

250 SPECIES OF DIFFERENT PLANTS IN THE PARK

35 THE NUMBER OF FOUNTAINS IN THE PARK

THE PARK IS HEART-SHAPED.

PARK LIFE

VILLA BORGHESE

Rome's most popular park has great views, museums, a zoo, a puppet show (see page 49), a tiny cinema, a boating lake, a train... and that's just for starters. Phew! You'll need a rest among its lovely trees and walkways once you've seen all it has to offer.

BIOPARCO BELLA FIGURA

The Bioparco zoo has over 1,300 animals to see from around the world (find out about their frozen fruit treats on page 61). They're not all behind fences. The zoo's free-roaming peacocks are well known for showing off their beautiful tails to photographers. They definitely rank highly among the image-conscious residents of Rome!

VILLA BORGHESE

HOW IT WAS NAMED

Around 500 years ago a wealthy cardinal called Scipione Borghese created the park for himself. He liked wine and wanted room for his own vineyards. His descendants added extras to it such as the lake and tree groves. Eventually it became a public space for everyone.

OLDER THAN THE ANCIENT ROMANS

THE VILLA GIULIA MUSEUM (ONE OF MANY MUSEUMS IN VILLA BORGHESE) IS FILLED WITH ETRUSCAN TREASURES. THE ETRUSCANS LIVED IN ITALY BEFORE THE ROMANS AND THEIR LIVES ARE MYSTERIOUS, THOUGH WE KNOW THEY WORE NOISY SHOES — AN ETRUSCAN WOOD AND METAL SANDAL IS ON DISPLAY IN THE MUSEUM.

AMONG THE ETRUSCAN TREASURES ON SHOW ARE THREE DELICATE LEAVES OF GOLD FOUND IN AN ANCIENT TEMPLE FROM 2500 BC. THEY ARE CALLED THE PYRGI TABLETS, AND THEY ARE MARKED WITH ITALY'S OLDEST-KNOWN WRITING — A DEDICATION TO A GODDESS CALLED ASHTARET.

IN ANOTHER OF THE PARK'S MUSEUMS (THE BORGHESE MUSEUM) THERE'S A TREE WITH A DIFFERENCE. IT'S A FAMOUS MARBLE STATUE BY BERNINI THAT SHOWS A MYTHICAL LADY CALLED DAPHNE TURNING INTO A TREE. HER FINGERS ARE BECOMING TWIGS AND LEAVES.

(MOSTLY) PRESIDENTS ONLY

QUIRINAL GARDENS

The public is only allowed into the formal gardens of the presidential Quirinal Palace on guided tours. But on one day of the year – Republic Day on 2 June – the garden is open free of charge. There, people can see the beautiful flower beds, trees, hedges and statues that are normally hidden in this VIP corner of town.

QUIRINAL GARDENS

FREE
FOR ONE DAY ONLY

OWLS EVERYWHERE

HOUSE OF THE OWLS

The Villa Torlonia is an unusual looking house in its own park. It was built for Prince Giovanni Torlonia, a wealthy banker in the 1800s. In the grounds he had a fairytale gingerbread-style house called Casina delle Civette (the house of the owls) built where he could escape for some downtime. He had it decorated with lots of owl images, though nobody knows why. It's a feathery mystery!

HOUSE OF THE OWLS

"Thanks, dear. Are there any biscuits?"

FREE SNACKS GROW HERE
VILLA DORIA PAMPHILI

Rome's largest park has rolling hills, lakes and plenty of beautiful stone pine trees. The stone pines are a symbol of Rome, and their delicious nuts have been eaten by locals for thousands of years. Ancient Roman soldiers packed them as snacks on journeys away from Rome. At the end of summer the trees drop their giant dry cones and it's time to collect the *pinoli romani*.

HILLTOP BATTLE SPOT

JANICULUM HILL

Each day, a cannon fires from this lofty spot to signal midday. It began firing in 1847, when Pope Pius IX wanted a signal to help synchronise all the church bells across town. The Janiculum was also the scene of a famous battle during the war to unify Italy. In 1849, Italian hero Giuseppe Garibaldi fought the French here, and there's a statue of him and his wife, Anita, who fought alongside him, on the hill. The story goes he would have morning coffee on the hill within view of the enemy to annoy them.

20M (66FT)
HEIGHT OF SOME OF THE TALLEST STONE PINES IN THE VILLA DORIA PAMPHILI PARK

PINE NUTS

SPECIAL CEMETERY

THE PROTESTANT CEMETERY

This cemetery for non-Catholics is far from gloomy. In fact it's world famous for its beauty, with its lanes of elegant gravestones, tall cypress trees and lots of lovely flowers. Many famous people, including authors and artists, have been buried here over its 300 years. Among its famous inhabitants are the English Romantic poets Keats and Shelley. When Keats died, Shelley wrote this about his resting place:

"It might make one in love with death, to think that one should be buried in so sweet a place."

PARCO SAVELLO

search: ROMAN ECO FACTS

📍 **GREEN ROMANS**

Rome hosted the International Conference on Geographical, Ecological and Environmental Sciences in 2017.

📍 **WHAT A WASTE!**

Since 2005, all Romans have to recycle – if they don't they face fines from €50 (£43) to €500 (£430)!

FRUIT CASTLE

PARCO SAVELLO

This park is also known as the *Giardino degli Aranci* (Orange Garden) because of the trees that grow there. According to legend, 800 years ago St. Dominic planted Italy's first orange tree next door at the Basilica di Santa Sabina. A descendant of that first tree still grows in the garden of the church. The park was once part of a medieval castle and it still has thick stone walls around it.

VILLA CELIMONTANA

ROSETO COMUNALE

COMPETITIVE PETALS

ROSETO COMUNALE

This rose garden has more than 1,000 rose varieties from all over the world. It stands on the site of a centuries-old Jewish cemetery and its pathways are laid out in the shape of a Jewish menorah (candelabra). Every spring one of the world's most important rose competitions, the Premio Roma, takes place here. The judges choose a winning rose species and it gets planted in the garden.

HIDDEN HAND

VILLA CELIMONTANA

Legend has it that something gruesome is underneath the Egyptian obelisk in this lovely park. It's the arm of a workman who lost it during an accident while setting up the obelisk in 1820. It was being lowered onto its stand when ropes broke and it crashed down.

MISSING

1 x ARM!

WALK, SHOP, WALK

Shopping can be a bit boring sometimes, but in Rome that's not the case because everywhere you look there's something interesting to see. Take a stroll and prepare for one of the most fascinating city shopping trips ever.

PIAZZA DEL POPOLO

START WITH ART

PIAZZA DEL POPOLO

You could start by making a shopping list sitting at one of the elegant cafés around this huge busy piazza, while you're entertained by street performers. It's been a popular spot for people watching for hundreds of years, but the entertainment hasn't always been so cheerful – public executions were once held here! In 2013 the piazza was partly filled with a huge floor canvas and everybody joined in to make a huge piazza picture. Brighter times!

START

STONE STREET

VIA MARGUTTA

This short street, now home of trendy galleries and art studios, has definitely got a lot smarter since Ancient Roman times when it was a stinky open sewer! You can get your own piece of Rome marble inscribed at one of its little shops, called the Bottega del Marmoraro (it means the shop of the marble mason). Its walls are lined with ancient stonemasons' tools.

VIA MARGUTTA

SIT DOWN ON THE STEPS

SPANISH STEPS

Rome's most famous staircase is always a good spot to sit down and have a rest. Artists often sit at the top of the steps drawing visitors' portraits. In spring it's lined with colourful pots of flowers, but in 2008 it was covered in hundreds of thousands of multicoloured plastic balls as an art protest.

138 THE TOTAL NUMBER OF STEPS

€1.5 MILLION (£1.32MILLION) AMOUNT SPENT RESTORING **THE STEPS IN 2016**

VIA DEL CORSO

SPANISH STEPS

STROLL STREET

VIA DEL CORSO

This long, straight shopping street is a favourite place for the *passeggiata*, the traditional evening stroll. Rome's inhabitants like to take a *passeggiata* (a little walk) between 5pm and 7pm before dinner to show off their best clothes. It's particularly popular at weekends, when families and friends take to the street to strut their stuff.

search: ANCIENT ROMAN MONEY MAKERS

HEY BIG SPENDER

The Ancient Romans borrowed the idea of coins from the Greeks. Emperors put pictures of themselves on coins to make themselves more popular. When they had spent too much, emperors reduced the amount of silver they put in coins by half.

I'LL HAVE A PINOCCHIO, PLEASE

BARTOLUCCI, VIA DEI PASTINI

This shop is filled with wooden toys, including handcrafted wooden Pinocchios, cuckoo clocks, swords and even a life-size carving of a motorbike.

PINOCCHIO IS A CLASSIC ITALIAN CHILDREN'S BOOK CHARACTER — A LITTLE WOODEN BOY WHO MAKES MISTAKES BUT REDEEMS HIMSELF TO BECOME A REAL BOY. HE WAS CREATED BY ITALIAN AUTHOR CARLO COLLODI IN 1881.

TOP TOYSHOP

AL SOGNO, PIAZZA NAVONA

This historic toyshop is famous for its incredible window displays. Inside it's a wonderland of dolls, puppets, fairies, trolls, elves, dolls' houses and amazing soft toys. Here you can buy a life-size polar bear, a panda or even a giraffe that will reach your bedroom ceiling. The shop's name translates as 'in a dream'.

PIAZZA NAVONA

* ON THE LIST *

MANY OF ROME'S MARKETS SPECIALISE IN DELICIOUS LOCAL FOOD SUCH AS CHEESE, MEAT AND VEGETABLES. HERE'S A LIST OF ITALIAN TREATS TO LOOK OUT FOR AT THE MARKETS AND AT LOCAL DELIS, TOO.

MOZZARELLA
CHEESE MADE FROM WATER BUFFALO MILK

PROSCIUTTO
A TASTY CURED (PRESERVED) HAM

PARMIGIANO REGGIANO
SALTY HARD CHEESE THAT'S GREAT GRATED OVER PASTA

POMODORI
YUMMY LOCAL TOMATOES THAT ARE SUPER-TASTY

MAIN MARKET
PORTA PORTESE MARKET

Rome has lots of street markets, but this mammoth Sunday flea market is the biggest, busiest, noisiest one of all. It has thousands of stalls selling all sorts of things, from international artisan clothes to electrical goods. The stallholders like to haggle loudly with their customers.

PORTA PORTESE MARKET

TESTACCIO

AMAZING MURALS
JUMPING WOLF IN TESTACCIO

On your way home with a bagful of tomatoes, a life-size stuffed toy, a piece of marble, a Pinocchio and an artist's portrait, you might come across some of Rome's street art. It's not all ancient sculptures and fountains. There are lots of modern murals, too, some of them covering whole buildings. One of the most striking is the mural of a wolf painted on the side of a block of flats in the lively Testaccio district.

BRILLIANT BUILDINGS

Many buildings around the world are modelled on Rome's ancient architecture. Become a construction detective and spy out the secrets of the city's structures. Then you'll be able to spot echoes of Rome in other cities and towns you visit.

START

EUR

HOUSE OF STYLE

PALAZZO DELLA CIVILITA ITALIANA, EUR

The Ancient Romans were the first builders in the world to create above-ground arches on their buildings. Twentieth-century architects copied them to design this stylish 1930s building. It is nicknamed the Square Colosseum. Its unstylishly long full name means the Palace of the Italian Civilization. It's now the oh-so-cool headquarters of Italian fashion house, Fendi.

VN POPOLO DI POETI DI ARTISTI DI EROI
DI SANTI DI PENSATORI DI SCIENZIATI
DI NAVIGATORI DI TRASMIGRATORI

THE LATEST THING 2,000 YEARS AGO

PYRAMID OF CAIUS CESTIUS

Why is there a pyramid in the middle of Rome's traffic? It's the result of a fashion in Ancient Rome for all things Ancient Egyptian. A local politician called Caius Cestius had his tomb built in what was then the latest style. It would once have been covered in shining marble for extra look-at-me effect.

PYRAMID OF CAIUS CESTIUS

BAROQUE ROME
BORROMINI'S PERSPECTIVE

In the 1600s, Rome went mad for Baroque, a style that was dramatic and exciting, with clever perspective and decorative flourishes. Bernini (see page 19) and Borromini are the designers who turned Rome Baroque. Borromini created this famous optical illusion at the Palazzo Spada, to delight and astonish everyone. It looks like a really long corridor but it's only 9m (29.5ft) long. It tricks the eye because the columns decrease in height and the floor slopes.

TEMPIETTO DI BRAMANTE

RENAISSANCE ROME
TEMPIETTO DI BRAMANTE

This small round chapel is claimed to be one of the first great buildings of the Renaissance, a time in the 1400s and 1500s when architects, sculptors and artists copied the Ancient Roman buildings, statues and frescoes being rediscovered around Rome. It has Roman-style columns, a dome and arches. It stands in a church courtyard on the site where it's said that the apostle St. Peter was crucified.

TEMPLE FOR ALL

THE PANTHEON

The Ancient Romans were the first people to build domes. In later centuries architects around the city and all over the world copied them. The Pantheon is the oldest surviving dome in the world. It's a fantastic feat of clever engineering.

BUILT FOR GODS

The name Pantheon means 'all the gods'. It was built as a temple to all the gods of Rome. In AD 609, it was turned into a Christian church. It's now the Basilica di Santa Maria ad Martyres. The famous Renaissance artist Raphael is buried here along with Italian kings and queens.

VEGGIE INSPIRATION

The building was first created by a Roman VIP called Marcus Agrippa. His name is on the inscription on the front. It was later rebuilt by the emperor Hadrian. He is said to have got the idea from looking at a pumpkin.

MODERN MARVEL

The dome was the very latest in modern architecture when it was created between AD 118 and 125. It appears to have no support, but actually the arches holding it up are hidden in the Pantheon walls. It was made of concrete cast on a wooden frame and its hollow spaces (called coffers) help to make it lighter. The Romans were the first to invent strong concrete by mixing mortar with sand.

THE PANTHEON

OCULUS
9M DIAMETER (29.5 FEET)

PANTHEON DOME
43.3M X 43.3M
(142 FEET X 142 FEET)

DIAMETER = HEIGHT

6M THICK WALLS (20 FEET)

THE OCULUS

I SPY COLUMNS

THE FRONT OF THE PANTHEON HAS GIANT COLUMNS SUPPORTING A PORCH CALLED A PORTICO. THEY ARE CORINTHIAN COLUMNS, NAMED BECAUSE OF THE WAY THE TOP PART OF THE COLUMN (THE CAPITAL) IS DESIGNED. HERE'S YOUR GUIDE TO SPOTTING COLUMNS BASED ON THE BUILDINGS OF ROME:

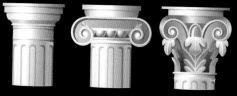

Doric **Ionic** **Corinthian**

ALL ABOUT MARBLE

THE ROMANS LOVED TO BUILD WITH MARBLE AND, IN LATER CENTURIES, THE MARBLE THEY USED WAS RECYCLED TO DECORATE MANY OF THE CHURCHES AROUND TOWN. MARBLE IS CREATED WHEN ROCKS GET SQUEEZED AND HEATED INSIDE A VOLCANO. THERE ARE LOTS OF DIFFERENT COLOURS, DEPENDING ON THE IMPURITIES IN THE ROCK THAT'S HEATED. LOOK OUT FOR THESE EXAMPLES:

Carrara **Pentelic**

Verde antico **Rosso antico**

TRAJAN'S

"I'm exhausted. Fancy a drink?"

MAXXI

TODAY'S ROME

MAXXI

This striking, contemporary building was designed by star architect Zaha Hadid. It houses Rome's premier contemporary art museum. It doesn't look Ancient Roman, but perhaps the ancients might have appreciated its geometric shapes, metal columns and steps. The Renaissance and Baroque designers would probably have covered up with all sorts of elaborate decoration!

THE FIRST MALL

TRAJAN'S MARKETS

The Ancient Romans built high-rise buildings, with shops on the ground floor and houses and offices behind and above. This big three-storey semi-circle was one of the world's first shopping malls with added offices and apartments – a 2,000-year-old version of what we see in modern towns. Now it's just another ancient ruin.

TRAJAN'S MARKETS

search: **ANCIENT ARCHITECTURE**

Ancient Roman architects developed things like:

amphitheatres – to provide the space for popular entertainment, like audience-led TV shows today

aqueducts – to move water (like modern plumbing)

domes – to amaze, they are still used in cathedrals, mosques, palaces and to cover indoor rainforests!

MODERN DREAMWORLD
RAINBOW MAGICLAND

In Rome's theme park, 20 minutes outside the city, anything goes. It is full of enchanted-looking buildings entirely based on the magical world of the imagination. There's a fairy school, a wizard's madhouse, a ghost ship and even a mysterious castle that hides a super-speedy rollercoaster.

QUARTIERE COPPEDÈ

FANTASY FUN
QUARTIERE COPPEDÈ

This small Rome neighbourhood has its own fairytale architecture. There are buildings with turrets, swirly sculptures, Arabic arches and scary gargoyles. This fantasy style is called Art Nouveau, and was popular when the buildings were designed in 1919 by the architect Gino Coppedè.

RAINBOW MAGICLAND

ROME'S GHOSTIE GUESTS

Rome has played such a big part in history it's no wonder that there are lots of ghosts rumoured to be hanging around. Dare you meet them on a night-time stroll? See if you can make it to a mysterious magic door at the end of the trail, without shivering!

NERO'S GHOST

CHIESA DI SANTA MARIA DEL POPOLO

Wicked Roman emperor Nero was said to be buried where this church now stands. His tomb lay near a wood of poplars (hence the name *del popolo*), next to a particularly spooky nut tree filled with sinister black crows. After locals complained that his ghost was partying round the nut tree with witches and devils, the pope had it cut down in 1099 and built a chapel on the spot. But has it stopped Nero's ghost hanging around? Some say noooooooooooo!

HAUNTED HANDPRINTS

MUSEUM OF THE HOLY SOULS IN PURGATORY

This tiny museum showcases objects said to have been 'branded' by the souls of people in purgatory (a kind of waiting room in the afterlife between heaven and hell, according to Catholic beliefs). When the collection was made in the 1800s it was thought that the souls of the dead had to stay in purgatory to atone for their sins, but they could get to heaven more quickly if their loved ones prayed for them on Earth. So it was believed that some souls came back and left handprints on objects such as clothes, table tops, books and hats, to get their loved ones to pray harder for them.

START

CHIESA DI SANTA MARIA DEL POPOLO

MUSEUM OF THE HOLY SOULS IN PURGATORY

SPOOKY SNUFF SNIFF

CASTEL SANT'ANGELO

The ghost of Mastro Titto, Rome's official executioner between 1796 and 1865, is said to wander the area around the castle in his scarlet cloak. Sometimes he stops passers-by and offers them a pinch of snuff, just as he once did to those condemned to die. His cloak and snuff box are on display at the Museo Criminologico (see page 38).

NO HEAD FOR HEIGHTS

PONTE SANT'ANGELO

The headless ghost of Beatrice Cenci is said to haunt this bridge on the night of 10 September. Beatrice and the rest of her family were beheaded here on the morning of 11 September 1599 after she murdered her father in one of 16th-century Rome's most notorious crimes. Her father was a cruel torturing tyrant, so many thought the executions were unfair and accused the pope at the time of ordering the multiple deaths to snatch the family's fortune. The sword used for the beheadings is on display in the Museo Criminologico.

PALAZZO DE CUPIS

DON'T WAVE BACK!

PALAZZO DE CUPIS

On moonlit nights, a ghostly hand is said to appear at a window of the Palazzo de Cupis. It once belonged to a lady called Costanza Conti de Cupis, who lived here in the 1600s. Her hand was so beautiful that an artist made a model of it, but one day a stranger saw the model and predicted that Costanza would soon lose her hand. Terrified, she hid indoors to stay away from harm, but one day she pricked her finger while sewing. Her arm became badly infected from the prick and she eventually had to have her hand cut off, though it didn't save her. She died but her hand is said to haunt her home.

BUMPS IN THE NIGHT

57 VIA DEL GOVERNO VECCHIO

Something weird went wild in this house in 1861, according to reports from the time. There were loud thuds and objects were thrown through the air and smashed against walls. Eventually the terrified owners left, though not before a number of eyewitnesses, including police officers, confirmed the mysterous goings-on. It sounds like the work of poltergeists, the messiest ghosts going. *Aiuto*! (Help!)

FICTIONAL PHANTOM

The world's first-known ghost story was written by Ancient Roman author Pliny the Younger. It tells of a man who buys a house at a bargain price, only to find a noisy, chain-rattling ghost popping up to bother him inside. Later a chained skeleton is found buried in the courtyard and after giving it a proper burial, the haunted homeowner finds peace at last.

CARRIAGE FULL OF COINS

PONTE SISTO

The ghost of Olimpia Maidalchini, the sister-in-law of Pope Innocent X, is said to ride across this bridge in a black carriage, carrying crates of gold coins and laughing like a witch. In life, she was the pope's advisor in the 1600s and was hated by locals, who nicknamed her the *Pimpaccia* (wicked woman) because they thought she made herself very rich at everybody's expense. When her protector, the pope, lay dying, she knew she was in danger from her enemies so she escaped Rome in her black carriage, taking the pope's treasure boxes with her. She died of the plague two years later.

PONTE SISTO

PIAZZA VITTORIO EMANUELE

DARE YOU KNOCK?

PIAZZA VITTORIO EMANUELE

A mysterious spooky-looking door flanked by two strange figures is all that remains of a villa where the Marquis Palombara lived in the 1600s. The story goes that the marquis once met an alchemist who told him he knew how to turn ordinary metal into gold. The next day the alchemist had disappeared but he had left behind some gold flakes and gold-making instructions, written in symbols that nobody could read. The marquis had the instructions carved on his doors in the hope that a passer-by would understand it and knock, but nobody ever did.

The weird symbols above the door still mystify visitors.

INDEX

INDEX

FURTHER READING

Horrible Histories: Rotten Romans
by Terry Deary and Martin Brown

Go back in time to visit the Ancient Romans in all their grottiest glory. This book celebrates all that is most fun and foul in this historic city.

Eyewitness Ancient Rome
Dorling Kindersley

This book is perfect for school projects on Ancient Rome – it's full of information about emperors and gods as well as everyday Romans.

The Cities Book
Lonely Planet Kids

This worldwide travel guide aimed at kids is crammed with really useful information on lots of cities, including Rome.

Michelangelo for Kids: His Life and Ideas, with 21 Activities
by Simonetta Carr

Find out all about the artistic genius and the Renaissance, then learn some of his techniques. Maybe you could create your own masterpieces after completing all the activities in this book!

The Thieves of Ostia
by Caroline Lawrence

This children's novel brings Ancient Rome alive as it follows a young dectective and her group of friends all around Rome uncovering secrets and solving mysteries.

The Orchard Book of Roman Myths
by Geraldine MacCaughrean and Emma Chichester Clark

Packed full of Ancient Roman myths that describe how Rome was created and who the Roman gods and goddesses were in a simple way that all children will love.